BEDSIDE REA ER SERIES

DEADWOOD SAINTS AND SINNERS

BY JERRY L. BRYANT
AND BARBARA FIFER

DEDICATION

To all that we have lost in Deadwood through greed and misguided attempts at renewal and to the many who have strived to collect all the resulting pieces, restore, and protect them.
J. L. B.

To Cynthia Weatherhead Ahlberg, Susanne Nicklet Bjorner, and Sherry DiBagno Brown, who always support the work and are there when the black dog comes running.
B. F.

ISBN: 978-1-56037-646-0

For more information about our books, write Farcountry Press, P.O. Box 5630, Helena, MT 59604; call (800) 821-3874; or visit www.farcountrypress.com.

Library of Congress Cataloging-in-Publication Data

Names: Bryant, Jerry L., 1945-2015, author. | Fifer, Barbara, author.
Title: Deadwood saints and sinners / Jerry L. Bryant, Barbara Fifer.
Description: Helena, MT : Farcountry Press, 2016. | Includes bibliographical references and index.
Identifiers: LCCN 2015038984 | ISBN 9781560376460 (alk. paper)
Subjects: LCSH: Deadwood (S.D.)--Biography. | Deadwood (S.D.)--History. | Frontier and pioneer life--South Dakota--Deadwood.
Classification: LCC F659.D2 B79 2016 | DDC 978.3/91--dc23
LC record available at http://lccn.loc.gov/2015038984

Produced and printed in the United States of America.

20 19 18 17 16 1 2 3 4 5 6

TABLE OF CONTENTS

THE CAMPS OF 1875-1876

J. L. Bryant

In the beginning there was a series of bustling mining camps situated in the gulches or steep canyons of Deadwood and Whitewood creeks. Their grouping forms something of loop when plotted on a map. The number and names of these camps and their relative importance to the "Gold Rush" is a matter of some conjecture, but my perception is this: The earliest camp in the "Loop" was Gayville. It was established in 1875 by Alfred and William Gay. It was located on Deadwood Creek near the confluence of False Bottom Creek, about one and a half miles west by southwest from the confluence of Deadwood and Whitewood creeks. Standing in Gayville looking north, the mountain you see is Gay Mountain, after William Gay.

Traveling north by northwest to the confluence of Deadwood and Whitewood creeks, the original camp of Deadwood was located on the north side of the creek, just east of the confluence.

On the south side of the creek was South Deadwood. Approximately a half mile northeast of the confluence was Elizabethtown. One quarter of a mile due east of Elizabethtown was Fountain City. Two tenths of a mile northeast of Fountain City was Whoop-up, within the margin of Spruce Gulch. Seven tenths of a mile east by northeast of Whoop-up was Montana City, at the confluence of Whitewood Creek and Split-tail Gulch.

That covers approximately one third of the "Loop" of early mining camps. The map shows their locations as best can be determined.

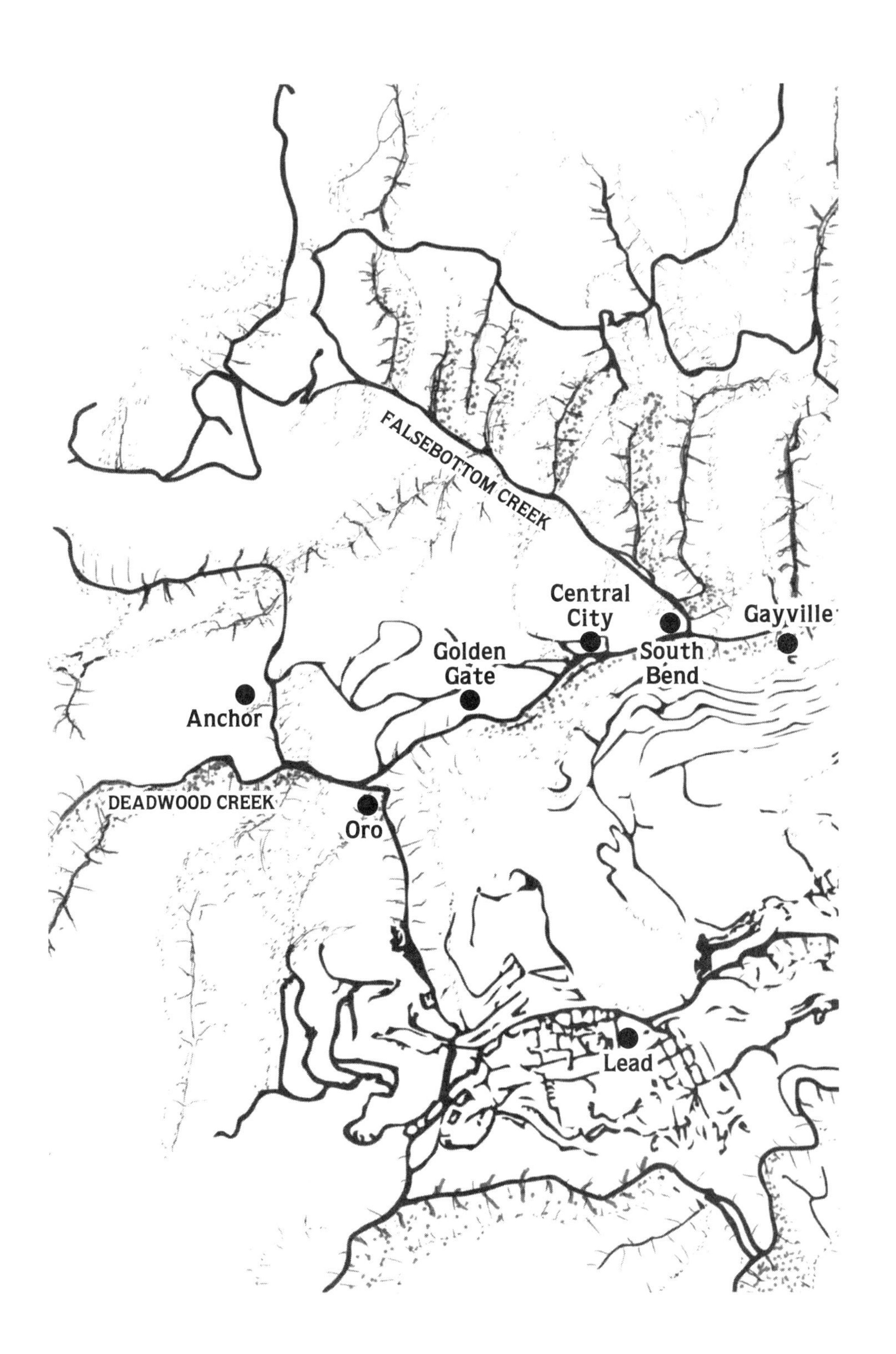
FALSEBOTTOM CREEK
Central City
Gayville
Golden Gate
South Bend
Anchor
DEADWOOD CREEK
Oro
Lead

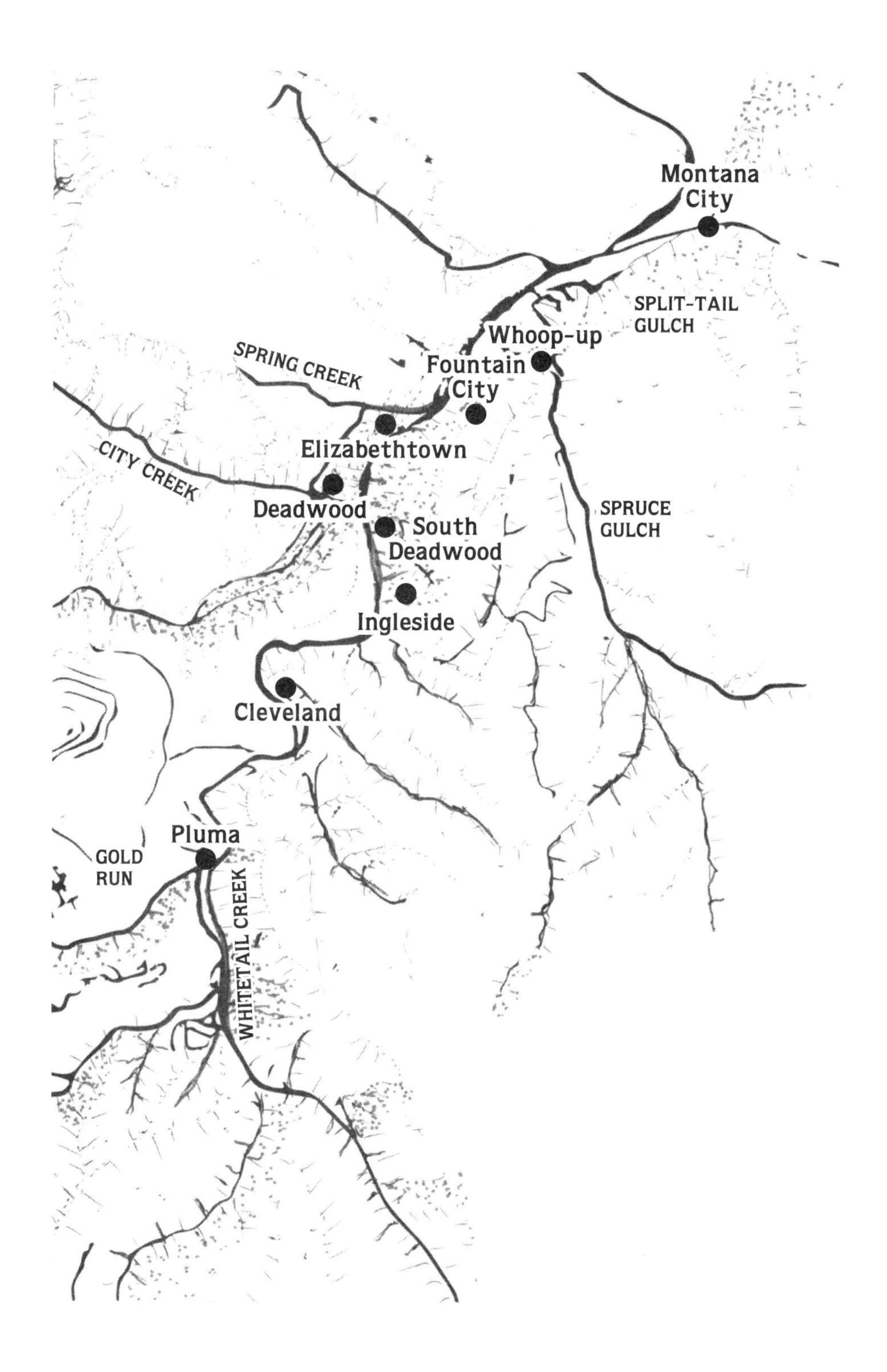
Montana City
SPLIT-TAIL GULCH
Whoop-up
SPRING CREEK
Fountain City
Elizabethtown
CITY CREEK
Deadwood
South Deadwood
SPRUCE GULCH
Ingleside
Cleveland
Pluma
GOLD RUN
WHITETAIL CREEK

CHAPTER ONE

BEFORE DEADWOOD: PEOPLE COME AND GONE

Be ye wary, all who enter the Black Hills thinking that the first whites here were members of that infamous army expedition led by Colonel Custer, who announced "gold at the grassroots" to a depression-plagued nation!

The question of who besides the Sioux was in the Black Hills before Custer and the gold rush seems not to tantalize my fellow researchers as much as it does me. Oftentimes, when I bring it up during conversations, I am smiled at and generally treated as though I have just slid into senility. But, barring any fits of dementia, I will argue that there were in fact Euro-Americans in and out of the Hills considerably before the arrival of Custer. First, we shall look at just a few instances that come down to us from the history books, and then, we will peruse the Deadwood newspapers.

I am not interested only in the famous (or infamous) of Deadwood's early days. I want to know who made this camp, this village, click—not only the one percent who had all the beans, or the nasties who made all the noise, or the ones dumb enough to play cards in Deadwood and not place their backs to wall.

The Black Hills did not just fall from the sky in 1874 to satisfy Custer's need for a road trip, they have been here all along. Is it too farfetched to wonder if perhaps the Spanish may have made it this far north? The Spanish were most definitely in Colorado. In 1743, the French Canadian brothers Chevalier and Louis La Verendrye explored much of Dakota, leaving a seven- by eight-inch plate at the location of present-day Pierre. Their journal suggests that they may have been at Bear Butte, about six miles northeast of present-day Sturgis. It is also a pretty well-accepted fact that Jedediah Smith crossed the Black Hills from east to west in 1823, and I find it very difficult to imagine that the fur trade stayed completely out of the Black Hills. We are speaking about mountain men, traders, and trappers, men who prided themselves in their abilities to know the land and to see new places. In the 1850s, Jim Bridger came to the Black Hills as a guide for a British hunting expedition. Sir St. George Gore, a wealthy, royal, absentee Irish landlord, came to the West with the purpose of shooting everything that moved. On the hunting party's route to Yellowstone, one of Gore's men found some gold in a creek. Sir St. George looked at the specimen and tossed it back into the stream, stating that it was nothing and pushing the men to move on. He did not want a perfectly good hunting trip ruined because his men decided to look for gold. At the approximate location of modern-day Sundance, Wyoming, Gore met a real Sioux chief and his warriors. The chief, Bear's Rib, was upset at finding white people on Sioux sacred ground, land that the Great Father in Washington had said would be theirs for eternity. Bear's Rib, not being an unreasonable man, gave them a choice; fight and die or give up everything they had. So Sir St. George and his men gave up everything, including their clothes, socks, and boots. With the wagons, the horses, the guns, and the food gone, the men became the first white folks to walk halfway across Dakota Territory in the nude. At a later date, a military mapping and exploration expedition led by Lt. G. Warren also met with Bear's Rib and his warriors. Warren was a little better prepared for the encounter than Gore had been, so he was merely asked to leave the Black Hills and stay out of them. Warren noted in his journal that Bear's Rib was still in possession of several of Gore's horses.

Perhaps the earliest clue that others preceded the gold rush into the Black Hills was an insignificant article in the *Black Hills Pioneer* from June 1876, which was titled "Old Mine."[1] The mine was discovered while men

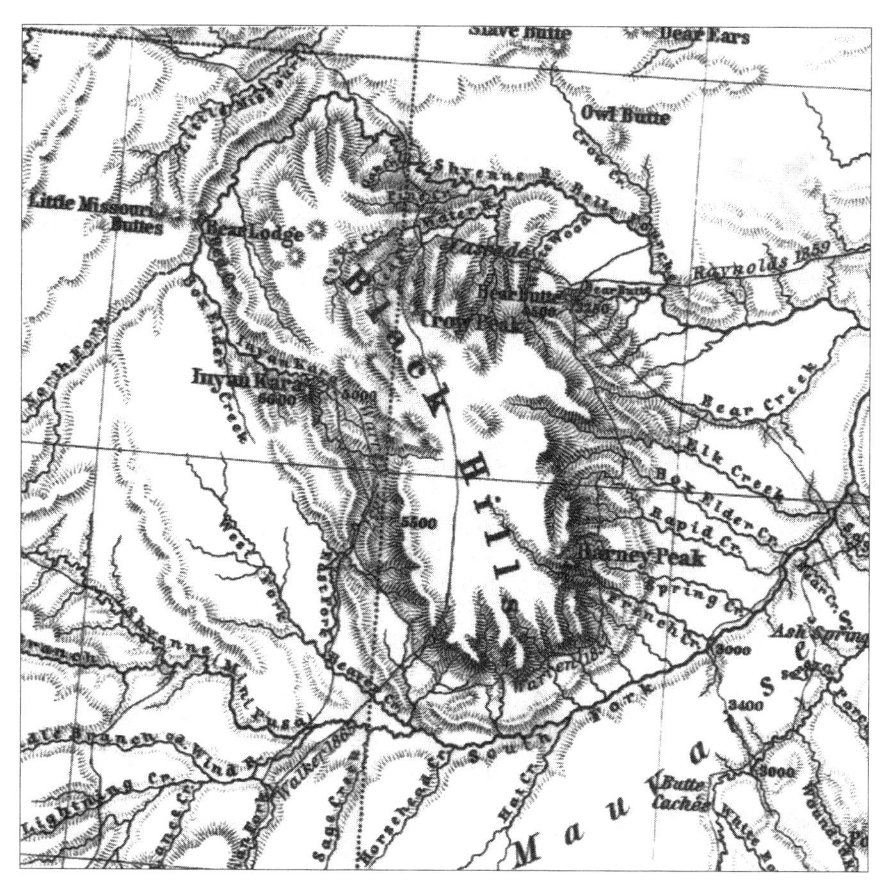

An 1875 atlas published in Germany shows not only the many waterways of the Black Hills but also the routes of early survey parties and military forays, including Warren in 1857, Raynolds in 1859, and Walker in 1865. Enlarged from World Atlas, *Adolf Stieler,* "Vereinigte Staaten Von Nord-Amerika, 1875."

were prospecting on the Yellow Jacket Claim. It was described as a drift that "had just struck the lead, when their work and their lives was brought to a tragic end." Small trees were growing up in the overburden pile, and the large trees around the opening of the drift were full of bullets. The claim belonged to Coleman and Anderson who had discovered it only the week before and believed that miners had opened the drift at least twenty years previously, prior to 1856.

That August came perhaps the most blood chilling of discoveries, when the bones of a man were discovered chained to a log on False Bottom

Creek. It appeared to the discoverers that the body had also been burned, sometime in the past, by Indians. The *Pioneer* editor stated that he was not sure if there was any truth to the story, but he printed it anyway.[2]

Eleven months later another clue was published in the newspaper. It originated from the least likely of sources, the Gem Theatre. Dick Brown and some of his cronies were working behind the Gem Theatre digging the foundation for a new smoke house. According to everyone in town, that area had not been dug down to bedrock. In other words, it was as undisturbed as creek dirt could be in 1877 Deadwood. Approximately eight feet below the surface, the diggers ran into what appeared to be the remains of an old mining camp. There was also a pair of very rusty iron gads (pointed tools, such as spikes or chisels, used for breaking up rocks or ore). The artifacts ended up on the *Times* editor's desk, where he pondered them for a while and wrote: "... a pair of iron gads that indicate by their bent and worn appearance that they did good service. They have evidently been buried very many years, as the rust holes that perforate them plainly show. As they lay upon our table, they seem like silent advocates, telling in their own mysterious way of the labor, hardship and privation of some ancient pioneers, who never reached civilization to unveil those hidden mysteries."[3]

Thus in the first two years of Deadwood newspapers we have pinpointed several temporal anomalies that have so far been ignored or disregarded by Black Hills historians. The year 1878 drags in a plethora of clues that also have also been summarily swept under the proverbial historical carpet or completely dismissed as being unfounded.

The first of these is a short article explaining that two men named Argue and Riley were hydraulicking on Claim No. 2 in Sawpit Gulch when they unearthed a "long handled wooden sluice fork" from near bedrock. The artifact was very heavy, being made of hardwood, and in an excellent state of preservation. It had been lying under five or six feet of gravel, and the men thought it had been there a very long time.[4]

Shortly, the *Black Hills Pioneer* became convinced that white people had been in and out of the Black Hills and mining gold for a very long time, citing a child's slipper that was found at the bedrock level. It appears that a man named Creighton had taken the shaft on one of his claims down to bedrock when he came across the slipper. The item was said to look like an ancient pattern and was verging on petrification. Intriguingly, some eighteen months before, several miners had been working on the hill above the Father DeSmet lode. The men were cutting timbers and found an ax-hewn log. When they tried to lift it to take it with them, the log disintegrated from rot.[5]

The *Times* also told the story of a Colt revolver that was found in one of the placer mines operating on Deadwood's Main Street in 1877. The gun was given to the *Times* editor, who started making inquiries at the Colt factory. Mr. W. E. Webster of Colt replied that a firearm with an identical serial number (11293) was sold by that company in 1853. The *Times* came to the conclusion that "This instance and others are proof conclusive that the existence of gold in the Black Hills is not a recent discovery and that at least 25 years ago mining was carried on here. The theory that the revolver was lost by a hunter and not a miner is not tenable, as it was found on bedrock in what may have been at that time a drainage ditch; whereas had it been lost by a hunter it would have lying nearer the surface."[6]

The next proof was revealed by Benjamin Charlton, Deadwood's forty-four-year-old court bailiff. Like most men in the Black Hills, Charlton spent his spare time prospecting, looking for the bonanza that would retire him from the work force forever. In mid-September of 1878, Charlton was prospecting about three miles north of Deadwood on a hill above Poland Creek when he happened across an amazing discovery.

On the hillside was an open cut running about thirty feet into the hill. The walls of the cut were eroded; the floor was well sodded over with trees growing in it. Nearby, Charlton found several trenches, three feet in depth and from fifteen to forty feet long. It appeared to Charlton, as the *Times* reported, that the early miners were mining cement ore, which they indeed had found, based on the contents of their waste rock piles.[7]

Charlton's discovery must have awakened a sleeping editor in the *Black Hills Pioneer* office because the very next day they published a long article titled, "The Black Hills Mystery—ancient mining camps, sluices, kettles and human bones found three years ago." This time the source of new evidence came from afar—Kansas City. The *Kansas City Times* had sent a special correspondent to the southern Black Hills and he reported an ancient mining camp or settlement that he had come across on French Creek near Calamity Peak. The correspondent noted that the remains of the camp appeared to be considerably older than those left behind by the Tallant Colony near Custer City. The article continued with information taken from the *Sioux City Journal* about the account of a "Kansas City Gentleman" who had scouted the Black Hills for several years with a party of four other men in 1863. During one of their trips, they discovered remains of what appeared to be an early white man's camp. The area was littered with human bones, three skulls, the remains of several wooden boats, and the bones of at least two horses. The camp was a natural fortification, with large stone slabs set on edge to serve as a defensive wall. The bones were bleached white, which made the scouts believe that the final event in this camp had occurred at least a generation earlier.

Metropolitan newspapers stoked Americans' fever for gold with stories and illustrations, like this one originally published in Harper's, *that fed the frenzy.*

In the same article, the *Kansas City Times* presented what they considered impeccable evidence, again from their correspondent who visited the Hills in 1876. Colonel Tallant took the reporter to a site that he had discovered while the Tallant expedition was initially in the Black Hills, prior to being expelled by the army. Only a short distance from the Tallant Stockade on French Creek, Tallant pointed out to the correspondent a number of primitive sluice boxes that had been made by cutting the heart out of cottonwood logs. Several of these were in very advanced stages of decay. The site was littered with pieces of tin and iron, and the remains of two shovels. Remnants of an early shelter, in the form of a few pine poles leaning against a sheltering rock, were also observed, as well as a grave. The grave was adorned with a small, crude cross held together by rawhide. Near the cross was a brown piece of granite with the initials "J. M." and a date of "1846" engraved on it.[8]

In 1887, Louis Thoen was working near the base of Lookout Mountain near present-day Spearfish. To earn extra money for his family he had been quarrying sandstone and cutting it into building blocks. As he proceeded about his business, he discovered an engraved slab of sandstone. This stone slab has piqued the imaginations of generations of historians, students, and museum goers ever since. Housed at the Adams Museum like a rare gem, the stone has also fueled generations of controversy. Scratched upon one side of its surface is the following text:

> *Came to these hills in 1833 seven of us all died but me Ezra Kind*
> *DeLacompt Ezra Kind G.W. Wood T. Brown*
> *R. Kent Wm. King Indian Crow*
> *killed by Indians beyond the high hill got our gold June 1834*
>
> On the opposite side of the stone it read:
> *Got all of the gold we could carry our ponys all got*
> *by Indians I have lost my gun and nothing to eat and Indians*
> *hunting me.*

But the prevailing question to this day still remains: was the stone something that Louis Thoen produced on a sunny afternoon of boredom, or is it the real thing?

The final example to surface in the Deadwood newspapers comes from the summer of 1890, and this one has nothing to do with mining. While the grade was being set for the Deadwood Central Railroad, the graders on the portion along upper Whitewood Creek were often required to dig down as deep as six feet. It was during such an operation that an old-fashioned Colt revolver was uncovered on the bottom of the grade. The gun was covered with rust; all the chambers were empty, but its hammer was in the full cock position.[9]

Who were these people, and where did they all go?

CHAPTER TWO

A TRIP DOWN THE GULCH WITH BARKER, THE BLACK HILLS HERMIT

A newsman's early-day expedition out from Deadwood enlightened his readers on the area's natural wonders—and inspired author Jerry L. Bryant's own physical and research treks.

A Prologue and a Plea

A few years ago, while doing research on the various towns and camps around the "Golden Loop" in the northern Black Hills, I came across the following article, from the *Black Hills Champion*, July 8, 1877, describing a trip from Deadwood up Whitewood Canyon to Crystal Spring Cave. The article, while it gave me no new information about my target of Montana City, piqued my curiosity about "Barker, the Black Hills Hermit." Over time, I have recovered a small trickling of information on Barker, but just enough to keep me excited and searching; thus I appeal to readers in case anyone might contribute further information.

A real break came in the form of pages of an old photo album that

The hermit known as Barker stands in front of the cave that was his home for many years.

went up for sale on eBay. Among these was a photograph showing Barker standing in front of his cave. It was taken by Coules, who worked in the Deadwood area in the 1880s. I eventually purchased the photograph and then later discovered a different photo of Barker in the California State Archives. This view was also taken by Coules, and helped me to identify the exact location of Barker's Cave.

> *They told us it was not more than four miles from Deadwood to Crystal Spring Cave yesterday morning when we started out on horseback for a trip down the gulch for the benefit of our readers. We rode four miles down the road over a difficult trail, and inquired again. From that place our informer said it was six miles a little farther down; another person said it must be between seven and eight miles. The longer we rode the farther our destination seemed [to] be away.*
>
> *In no other part of this country can such grand and beautiful scenery be seen as a walk or ride down Deadwood Gulch. On each side, and in some places almost perpendicular for a great height, the bluffs loom overhead. In other spots, again, the ridge is indented*

Whitewood Creek, named for the aspen that line its banks, wends through the Black Hills.

with smaller gulches, and slopes gently down to the creek. The most luxuriant vegetation flourished on every hand. The ground is fairly covered with variously colored wild flowers, lending cheerful and happy appearance to the hillsides and valleys. The bottom of the gulch is turned topsey turvy in every direction by mining operations which are going on vigorously all the way down the creek. No heavy, brilliant strikes have been made, or are being made but the mines a yielding big wages to their owners, and in default of better production they are contented with this. Experienced miners tell us that the placer digging in Whitewood Gulch below Deadwood will hold out big pay yet for many years of steady work, notwithstanding the assertions to the contrary by dissatisfied croakers. Why, in a large number of mines which were deserted last year or only hurriedly worked there is considerable money being made this season by rewashing last year's tailing and sinking the shaft wider and deeper there is plenty of water in the creek, which can be gotten to any part of the gulch with very little trouble. Huts and cabins have sprung up thick on both sides and very comfortable and neat some of them are, too, considering the absence altogether of females in these places.

The miners trail down the gulch is a very rough uneven and round about sort of a concern it requires the utmost care of a foot passenger and a pony cannot possibly go down more than four miles, for which distance the trail was been worked a little. We were compelled to leave our horse tied before a cabin in the Cape Horn District of Airy Flat. The Cape Horn district receives its name from a high rocky bluff towering over the gulch giant-like. It is said to bear considerable resemblance to the great rock on the very point of Cape Horn, South America. On each side of Airy Flat the bluffs rise to an enormous height almost perpendicular, and the small even triangular shaped flat, called Airy, lies hemmed in on all side.

The entrance to the hermit's cave is northeast of Deadwood on Whitewood Creek.
PHOTOGRAPH BY JERRY BRYANT.

On the western side of Airy Flat is located Barker's Cave. Barker was one of the very first settlers in these Hills. He came here about as soon as anybody and stayed here until the present time, Indians and the government to the contrary notwithstanding; when he first came here he was bothered by the Indian very much. The "Reds" were after his scalp and he was legging it up over Airy Flat about as fast as a man generally goes under such circumstances. The Indians were almost upon him and he was just making up his mind to turn and fight for it when he espied the mouth of a small cave. In a second he had slipped in, turned on his pursuers, and let them have the contents of his gun full in their faces. The savages suddenly bethought themselves of some business they had on the other side of the rock and left immediately, carrying with them a severely wounded comrade. They kept Barker in his cave for several days, when he managed to elude them. Quite a number of times after this circumstance the cave proved handy to him for shelter from the weather and the

Soot on the ceiling and remnants of an old stove pipe hint at the hermit's primitive living conditions.

Indians. Finally he made it his home and claimed the spot. Here he lives to-day in his little cave, the honest, sturdy and brave pioneer. His claim is panning out big and he is now reaping the reward of his earlier bravery.

Loveland and Murray of Omaha and Sioux City respectively are putting up a large water power saw mill on Airy Flat at the head of Boulder Falls. Their capacity when in full running order, as they expect to be next Wednesday, will be 10,000 feet per day. Other buildings are in the course of erection on the flat and it promises to be quite a town by fall. A fine road has been constructed from Airy through a side gulch out to Centennial valley road.

Just below the Airy Flat is the Boulder Falls. These falls will compare in beauty and wild grand scenery with any spot in the west. For about 80 rods there is a fall of 215 feet in Whitewood Creek. Great rocks and boulders, the largest we have ever seen, lay helter skelter in the bed of the creek, damming it up in places so that it runs over the top and forms a series of miniature falls delightful in every respect. The rocks and boulders must have been thrown into their present situation by an earthquake or volcanic eruption. There are fissures in the rocky bluff, right over the falls to the left, going down which are 75 to 100 feet long, over three hundred feet and a foot and half in width. It makes the head dizzy to look into the dark yawning crevice stretching away down out of sight. The muddy mining creek rushes down the rocky canyon with a tremendous noise and the roar of the mad whirling waters can be heard from a great distance up and down the creek from the falls. The old trail leads right through the narrow canyon along side the falls it requires an expert climber and jumper to traverse it. But the traveler is amply repaid for his trouble by witnessing the great beauty of the minor falls and the dashing foaming water around his feet. The new trail is a little farther and easier and leads over the bluff. The yellow muddy mining water spoils the effect somewhat, but yet the sight is unequalled and well worthy the trouble to go see.

About two miles below Boulder Falls, we reach the final objective of our journey: Crystal Spring cave. It is on the right of the creek going down and about half way up a five or six hundred foot bluff. It took some tall climbing and scratching to get there and when we did reach the table rock directly in front of the mouth of the cave, there was not a thimbleful of wind left in us. We felt a good deal like sitting or dropping down but preferred to sit. After a rest of half an hour, in company with several others who had just arrived, we proceeded to make arrangements for a complete exploration of the cave. A number of pitch pine knots were cut and lit, and with hammers and chisels we started into the mouth of the cave. Inside the air was cold, damp and filled with smoke. Previous parties had been in and camped there, and the smoke from their fires still remained in the cave as evidence that there was no other outlet. At one time, as could be seen yet in many places, the roof and sides must have presented a grand glittering appearance, but the smoke has now blackened a greater portion of the walls and spoiled their looks. Long icicle like projections hang from the side and where smoke has not reached them or where dripping water has washed the blackening off, it is a beautiful sight indeed. The crystal quartz, of which the projections are composed, form a thousand and one different angles and sizes, and the light from the torches, reflected, send out all the varied colored rays of the rainbow, and the light is truly wonderful.

At its mouth, the cave is large enough for anybody to stand straight up in, but as we proceeded it began to grow smaller and smaller and we had to stoop half over in order to make any progress. We picked up some fine crystal quartz specimens, just here, which had fallen from the roof. For about 30 feet we walked along in a recumbent position, and then emerged into a vast vaulted hall. It must have been over 40 feet from the floor to the ceiling of this magnificent temple. It measured 30 feet across and 50 feet long. A pistol shot was fired here and the report was deafening, as its echoes rang again and again through the gloomy, growing fainter and fainter, and finally dying away in the distance. One of the party sang a song, and the effect was enchanting as the musical vibrations rolled through the empty cavern. We descended from the temple down a steep ridge and found ourselves in another room which was fully as long and as wide, but not so high as the temple. This is the most beautiful part of the cave, as the smoke has not done as much blackening, and the quartz shows clear and glittering in the light of the torches.

The cave now began to grow narrower, and we thought we reached the end; but on examination we found it stretched farther back and we had to get down on our hands and knees to proceed. We crawled along for some time in this shape, and it grew smaller and smaller and finally we had lay down and wriggled along as best we could. The dust and smoke, however, was so thick that we had to back out, and for want of time failed to go clear to the end. There is no doubt but what it opens into a larger room some distance on if a person could stand it to go on through. We calculated that we went into the cave to a depth of 300 feet.

It is a sight well worth seeing and will pay for the trouble taken.[1]

CHAPTER THREE

ADRIENNE DAVIS: A WOMAN AMONG THE MINERS

"If women continue to come here, Deadwood will soon be like any other Western town—all its picturesque lawlessness will disappear," Adrienne Davis told her readers of the New York Daily Graphic. *She was only too happy to describe the realities of Deadwood in 1877 —good or bad.*

A Woman among the miners.

The Experiences of a New York Belle in the Black Hills.

How Deadwood Compares with Gotham—
Prospects of the Mines.

It is with pleasure that we give to our readers the following extracts from the private letter of a lady now residing in Deadwood City, in the Black Hills. A few years ago she was the accomplished and courted belle of one of the very best circles of society in New York. Today she is living with her husband in what is perhaps the most uncivilized of our so-called mining cities. Her letter is well worth a place in our columns:

DEADWOOD, AUGUST 11 – Here I am in the Black Hills and to my surprise I find it quite pleasant. One sees plenty of character here, and people in New York can scarcely realize the immense difference in the inhabitants of the two places. It seems as if the two belonged to different nations, such is the change in appearance, habits, and even language, for the latter is at first hardly intelligible to a newcomer, such is the admixture of profanity and slang. I hear plenty of it, for my room is separated from the street only by the thinnest of board partitions, and so far as hearing goes, I enjoy "every possible facility."

It was but a few moments ago that a genuine Deadwooder rode into the livery stable next door and shouted, in a tone that went through and through the walls, his dissatisfaction at the steed hired thus: "Say, old fellow, is this the ass Christ rode into Jerusalem on? You can't play that on me. Rustle around, and saddle up that calico horse there, or I'll be blankety blanked if I don't put a *Mansard Roof* on you!" But this is very mild compared with what we hear every hour.

A "Rocksharp."

I have become quite a "Rocksharp" myself. Excuse me, but when you hear the term twenty or thirty times a day applied to any good judge of gold-bearing rock, the temptation to use it "for short" become[s] irresistible. I have learned here to become more lenient to people who do not confine themselves entirely to the *Webster's Unabridged*. When a country is new and lawless, the language will in some degree conform to the current sentiment and circumstances. It is then that lawless terms and characters both appear, and both have their day.

Well, as I was saying, I have become quite a "Rocksharp." In New York, any piece of quartz was to me but a dull, unmeaning, uninteresting piece of stone, but when you have learned to turn it over and over in hopes of detecting the least little bit of yellow gold imbedded in it, and realize that such a stone may pave the way to one's fortune, it begets a certain interest and even fascination.

Old arrastras and other ruins still dot today's Black Hills.

The Boss Room of Deadwood

The town is hastily put up and the houses are very primitive. A shelter from the weather is all that is required, and many can hardly attain that. The Irish cabins about Central Park are luxurious dwellings compared to many here. My room is relatively quite elaborate. Canvas has been tacked to the boards and then papered. This alone is more than equivalent to frescoed walls in town. Besides, we have put up curtains and put down Brussels carpet. We have arranged pictures, ferns, autumn leaves, and intend to upholster a lounge, so that, although it is but a nutshell of a room, and as hot as an oven when the sun beats down on the thin walls, still it has already become known as the "Boss Room" of Deadwood. Last evening I entertained two bankers, two judges, and a United States Senator. We hadn't chairs enough, so we made deposits of the two bankers on the bed, and passed a delightful evening. There are two or three houses here which have attained the dignity of plastered walls, and one boasts a piano, which is the very cap sheaf of luxury. The fare at our hotel table embraces plenty of game, such as venison and elk. We have had wild raspberries in plenty, and lettuce three times. But eggs, poultry, and a hundred other articles on your daily bill of fare, are as yet unheard of in Deadwood.

Running the Gauntlet

We had an exciting and perilous time getting here. Indians were reported all around us after leaving Hat Creek. At every ranch where we stopped "fresh trails" were reported. The last night of the journey we heard, as we thought, the cries all about us of coyotes, owls, or strange night birds, but we were much alarmed when told that these were Indians signaling each other. The stage was ploughing through heavy sand and the horse gait was reduced to a slow walk. Only two men were with us and every while the vehicle stopped, and one of those went forward to reconnoiter. There was this other lady and myself on board, and during these dreadful intervals we listened in dreary silence and darkness with our hearts in our mouths. We did not know whether the expected foes might turn out to be road agents or Indians. The first named we held as much lighter ill of the two, although we hid all our valuables in anticipation of a visit. But the Sioux, we were told have no mercy—especially for a woman. So the other lady and I resolved that we would kill ourselves rather than fall into their hands. We sat for hours in the darkness, startled at every sound, with our knives ready to use on ourselves should we be attacked by those fiends of the forest. You will soon get all the nursery and novel romance about the red man rubbed off in this country. I think one such night as I passed on that Deadwood stage would make one wish that Cooper had really buried the last of the Mohicans or any other Indian. All along the roadside the graves of those murdered by the Sioux are pointed out, and they are numerous. Well, we got through unmolested by robbers or Indians. There was not time enough given for us to laugh at our own fears either, as most folks will when apprehensions are not realized and nothing is suffered but fear—which is bad enough. And Why? Because the very next stage after us was robbed. Then it was only the other day, while our next-door neighbors were at Spearfish, a locality nine miles distant, looking after their cattle, that they were killed and scalped by the Indians, although they fought hard for three hours, after entrenching themselves. Indeed, these occurrences are so common that the older residents don't classify being killed by Indians as a casualty, but rather, as they remark, one of the natural diseases of the country.

Mining Prospects

Good judges think that the mines here will last. The mineral belt is limited, but what there is is very good, and much is yet to be discovered. Deadwood is a lively town, especially in the evening, when the numerous gambling houses, liquor Saloons, Stores and variety theatres and the bands of music playing, and the streets are filled with miners. "Pilgrims" and Tenderfeet," as the later arrivals from the States are called from the fact that that many of them are sore-footed from long tramping. Fast women are very plentiful, among whom "Calamity Jane" stands at the head. She recently assisted her male companions to rob a stage, then got them drunk, stole the plunder and escaped while they were captured. "Calamity Jane" rides on horse back without a side-saddle, is a good shot, and as a frontiers-woman is better than a good many men. *Adrienne*[1]

In the gulches of Deadwood, placer miners processed ore through flumes and arrastras powered by water wheels.

The Delights of Deadwood City. A sharp eyed woman tells what she sees and hears in the Black Hills

More Girls Wanted—A Miner's Matinee— Gold Dust For Small Change— Picturesque Ruffians

(Correspondence of the Graphic*)*

DEADWOOD, DAKOTA, SEPTEMBER 5 – We have plenty of excitement in Deadwood, as a general thing, but a week or two ago we were treated to a sensation hitherto unknown in our experience. Before we were out of bed, or perhaps I should say awake—for a number of our citizens spend their nights as well as their days on the sidewalks—messengers galloped into town with the startling announcement that Gayville was in flames. I ought to explain that about three miles above Deadwood another town exists, or rather a trinity of towns, consisting of one long street. The beginning of this street is called Gayville, the middle South Bend, and the end Central City. Each hopes in time to rival Deadwood, and is big in it's [sic] own importance, but Gayville, consisting of over a hundred buildings—Gayville's pretensions seemed at an end; Gayville was being destroyed by fire. We, in Deadwood, flocked to her assistance and offered sympathy, which is all we have to offer in such an emergency, for we have neither engine, hose nor anything else with which to fight the enemy. Against Indians or typhoid fever we are more or less prepared, but as it was we looked on helplessly, and in two hours saw Gayville reduced to ashes—a fate which sooner or later, will as surely overtake Deadwood.

Now mark our western enterprise! While the town was still burning, two men started on horseback and contracted for a new building to be ready for occupancy by night. The still-burning debris was cleared away, and by sunset those two enterprising citizens could be seen dealing liquid death to the miners, with all the routine of an enterprising dance hall again in progress. At the end of two weeks Gayville has risen like [a] phoenix from the ashes, a finer and better built town than her rival.

The Bell[e] of the Black Hills

Her neighbor, Central City, has the advantage of us all in one respect—she can claim, as a resident, the only young lady in the Black Hills. When I say young lady, I mean it in every sense of the word. She is eighteen, lovely, accomplished and charming. Her fame extends far and wide, and it is needless to say that she can have her choice of all the unmarried men in the Hills, and many of our young bankers, lawyers, and capitalists would be considered eligible anywhere. However, she turns a deaf ear to them all, and sighs over the ill fortune which wafted her family to this barbarous country. If some good, bright, sensible girl would make up her mind to come her[e], what splendid matrimonial opportunities she could have to choose from.

A Deadwood Matinee

Another sensational event has just occurred. Some twenty or thirty shots have just been fired in rapid succession. All Deadwood rushes into the streets to see what is the matter. A late passenger in the Cheyenne coach has recognized in a lounger one of the party who robbed the stage and relieved the passengers of their money and valuables, and this man in particular of $1,400. He commenced firing on the road agent; the fire was returned; others joined in. The robber seized a horse, mounted and started for the woods, firing right and left. His horse was shot; he jumped and ran, and was shot through the chest and taken. In the meantime, two of his companions made quietly for their horses and attempted to leave town unobserved, but were seen and also captured. All are now in jail, but will be taken to Cheyenne for trial, though everyone here thinks that Judge Lynch [a lynching, or hanging without a trial] will see that they don't get there. The wounded have been cared for, and the streets are yet filled with groups of excited men, discussing the late occurrence.

The chief of this band is a beardless youth known as "The Boy." It is hoped that the rest of the band will soon be taken. They have been a terror to the stage company for the last six months, and have successfully robbed many a stage.

A Traveling Armory

The company sends out its treasure now but once a week, and then the preparations for its protection are truly formidable. No passengers are taken, the center seat is removed, and a solid iron safe is bolted, barred, and riveted in its place. Armed messengers ride inside and out, and four soldiers accompany each stage. With these precautions they hope to send out safely the large amounts of gold which have been accumulating since the road agents first commenced their depredations.

Black Hills Legal Tender

Speaking of gold, I must tell you that gold dust is legal tender here in any amount, from five cents up, and it is amusing to see the ladies shopping with their bottles of gold dust, in place of dainty porte-monnaie [wallet] and crisp greenbacks. It takes some time to get accustomed to this currency, and even now I am not able to count my change. I am obliged to look wise and trust the honesty, or more often the dishonesty, of the shop keeper.

The Luxury of Being Clean

The Chinese have flocked here in great numbers and one sees their quaint signs all over town—Sam Sing, Wing Lee, Ok Kee, Kung Wa, and washing and ironing—and I must give my testimony that whatever they do, they do well. When I first arrived here I found that clean linen [underwear] was a luxury to be indulged in sparingly, but opposition in trade has finally reduced the price of washing to $3 a dozen, and from the appearance of most persons, I should judge that only the few could afford that.

A Chinese Party

Preparations for some festivity seemed to be in progress yesterday at a Chinese wash-house, within range of my window—a tea party or kettle-drum, I should suppose—for several gorgeously attired Chinese women severally wended there way there. They were arrayed in gay colored loose trousers, flow[ing] silk blouses, lined and face[d] with b[r]ight colors, gold pins and ornaments in their black hair, and the *tout ensemble*—bias eyes and bright silk kerchiefs on their heads—look precisely like the pictures one sees on a five cent fan. I hastily seized my opera glass (relic of civilization), and ensconced myself behind my curtains and gazed with intense interest while the tiny cups of tea were passed around, the various dishes of sweetmeats tasted, and lastly the opium pipe lighted and passed from mouth to mouth—till the chattering gradually grew less as they were in turn overcome with stupor. When they recovered from its effects they took their departure, chattering noisily, no doubt expressing themselves politely and volubly in Chinese concerning the charming time they had, and how much they were indebted to Mrs. Ok Kee for such delightful entertainment. There is a good deal of the same kind of humbug all over the world, I find.

Camp Oddities

There are a good many odd people here, and many nice people too. It takes all kinds to make a mining camp, you know—bakers, speculators, judges and capitalists, elbow miners, gamblers, people who have been in penitentiaries, and people who ought to be there. Butternut trousers, woolen shirts, and top boots are the prevailing style here, and any other costume is the exception. Among our notabilities I might mention "Trail Pete," or "Buckskin Charley"—an Englishman, whose name before he dissipated his immense patrimony and retired from civilization was Reginald Grant Dalton—"Toothpick Joe," and the Utter Boys, these last, two bearded desperadoes with auburn curls reaching far below their cartridge belts, and better known by the *soubriquet* of "the Sorrel-haired twins," and many others too numerous to mention. Most of these are restless spirits, who have been in every camp in America—California[,] Nevada, Idaho, Montana and Utah; they have all killed their man or two, fought Indians, faro, and starvation and now agree that "America is played out. Railroads, telegraphs, and such new-fangled notions have spoiled it. Too many people spreading 'round." And many of them are talking seriously of taking a prospecting trip to South Africa, not that anything particularly rich has been found there, but they must go somewhere out of civilization, and they have completely exhausted America.

A Deadwood Romance

To be successful in a mining camp requires a peculiar fitness for the life. Many of the large army of "tenderfeet" and "pilgrims" who flocked

THE DAILY GRAPHIC: NEW YORK, FRIDAY, OCTOBER 12, 1877.

THE METROPOLIS OF THE BLACK HILLS

GENERAL VIEW OF THE CITY OF DEADWOOD.

The New York Daily Graphic *entranced readers with reports from Deadwood.*

here from the East last spring, expecting to pick up nuggets of gold in the streets, have returned home disappointed and disgusted. Others still remain without the means of returning, and are willing to do anything to keep from starving. Among the many waiters at the Welch House here is a quiet, gentlemanly young fellow, whose refined face and manners show plainly his superiority to his occupation. After watching him attentively for a day or two, I startled him with the question, "How long have you been a waiter?" He flushed and replied, "Madame, this is my first experience." On making further inquiries I discovered that he was a college graduate, and belonged to a good and wealthy family [in the] East. His father failed, and he took charge of a high school in Elmira, N.Y. The Black Hills fever broke out, and he with others started for Deadwood to make a fortune. On his arrival he soon discovered that his luxurious student life had not fitted him for such an experience. He could find nothing to do, and as a last resource accepted the position of hotel waiter, hoping to earn enough in that capacity to enable him to retrace his steps home. He still takes my orders and serves my steak and coffee with a courtly grace better suited to a drawing room, and is gaining more experience of life and people than he ever dreamed of during his more prosperous days. I feel sorry for him, but his experience is only one of many here.

Significant Names of Localities

I have been amused at some of the queer names of the different mining localities here, yet some of them seem quite pathetic too. I give as an example: "Hungry Gulch," "Poor Man's Gulch," "Black Tail," "White Tail" and "Sheep Tail" gulches, "Dead Broke Mine," "[T]wo-bit Gulch," "Potato" and "Rutabaga" camps, "Nigger" and "Bear" gulches, "Last Chance Mine," ["]Shirt-Tail Gulch," ["]Home Stake Mine" and "Dead Man's Gulch." The names of all these are suggestive enough for the imagination to weave many a history for them.

Women's Influence

Many nice houses are being erected on the hills back of Deadwood—pretty white cottages with green blinds and plazas. A number of men have b[r]ought or intend bringing their families here—a sure sign of the permanency of a camp. A woman's influence is quickly felt in such a place as this. I can pick out every home where there is a woman by the improved look of the surroundings—the clean doorstep, the dainty shades and curtains, the attempt to cultivate some wild vines or plants, all betray a woman's presence. Now and then one sees a canary in its gilt cage and hears the prattle of children. All this does more to civilize a camp than a car-load of missionaries and bibles. Rough men stop swearing and apologize if a woman appears, though it is almost as natural for a miner to swear as to breath[e]. If women continue to come here, Deadwood will soon be like any other Western town—all its picturesque lawlessness will disappear.

The houses generally consist of three or four rooms all on one floor, and everyone does his own house work, sending the washing and ironing to the laundries. A few employ Chinese servants, but good servants are difficult to obtain, and wages are high–from thirty to forty dollars a month. The greater number of people here take their meals [at] some of the many hotels. The miner[s] cook for themselves, and live anyway [sic] they can. There is much illness here, occasioned by the water, which mining has rendered unfit for drinking. Every natural death that occurs here is from typhoid fever, and our doctors are few; I believe there are only two in the Hills. Of course the bad water is an excellent excuse for steady whiskey drinkers and for an occasional extra quart or two, and the liquor dealers are steadily getting rich, and they are numerous here, too.

Indians

Our greatest danger at present seems to be from the Indians. A report has just been heard from reliable sources [that] the Indians from the Red Cloud Agency threaten an outbreak. There are 10,000 Indians and only three companies of soldiers. If they attack the town we think we can defend ourselves, but if they go on the warpath and cut off our wagon trains of supplies they will soon reduce the camp to starvation. If the government would only spend six months in the Hills and learn the truly vile, treacherous, bloodthirsty nature of the Indian, I am sure the policy would be total extermination. Deadwood has offered a reward of $250 for every Indian Scalp taken. If the government would follow the same course, it would be a quicker and more successful way of "civilizing the Indians" and rendering the western territories habitable than any amount of Indian policy will ever do. A number of Indians will get a permit from one of the agencies for a month[']s hunting, then start out and steal stock and scalp every white man they can find. When the time[']s up they return to the agency to be fed, warmed, and blanketed, while another party takes their turn at the warpath and scalping.

Agriculture and Mining Resources of the Hills

But it is time I give you some facts relative to the mining and agricultural resources of this country. To commence with agriculture, I can only say that the Hills are surrounded by valleys that appear capable of producing anything that can be raised in the temperate zone. Farming is carried on to a very limited extent, and then merely as an experiment, which so far has proved successful. Potatoes, peas, cucumbers, melons, cabbages, squash, and other vegetables have been raised here of excellent size and quality. Grain crops would probably do as well. All the hay used is cut here in great quantities from wild grass. Many promising ranches have been abandoned for fear of Indians. However, mining seems to absorb all the attention in the Hills to the exclusion of everything else; one hears—quartz, quartz, and nothing but quartz talked from morning to night.

The gold belt of these hills extends in length about sixty miles, and forty in width. All over the extent of this country gold has been found in some quantities, but the only extensive producing belt is that in the immediate vicinity of Deadwood. The ore runs all the way from five to fifty [dollars] per ton, but the average yield is fifteen dollars a ton. There is a large number of mines containing immense quantities of ore yielding from four to eight dollars per ton, but cannot be profitably worked until larger stamp mills can be brought in, running from sixty to a hundred stamps. There are about thirty stamp mills here now, and more on the way, all varying from five to thirty stamps each. The ore is a free milling ore, and the mills save from eighty to ninety percent of the gold. The gulch mining generally pays well—all the way from 10 cents to $50 a day per man. Many gulches where gold is known to exist cannot be made available at present on account of the distance to bedrock, where the precious metal is found, and the impossibility without expensive pumping machinery. The gulches will not be worked out for some years yet, and then can be made profitable [b]y being worked over again by bed-rock flumes, such as were in use in California. The principle [sic] gold mines are the "Keets," "Aurora," "Hidden Treasure," "Fairview," "Golden Terra," "Father De Smet," "Home Stake," and "Old Abe." During the month of August the Black Hills produced and shipped over $400,000 in gold. This is the product of the month only, and the figures can be relied on. The banks are overrun with business—have more than they can attend to.

Silver Mines at Bare Butte

The silver belt, which is entirely distinct from the gold belt, is about eight miles long and two miles wide. The ore contains all the way from five to five thousand ounces of silver [per ton of rock] and forty percent lead. The principle [sic] mines are the "Yellow Jacket," "El Refugio," "Florence," "Treasure," and "Red Cloud." A smelting furnace for lead and silver ore has just arrived from Omaha, but it is too soon to speak of it as a success or failure—time will show.

In conclusion, I must say our territory possesses every element of success. The wealth is here requiring only patience and industry to realize it. *Adrienne*[2]

A Woman in the Black Hills
Everyday Experiences in the Land of Gold—
Robbers And Miners
New Enterprises, Good and Bad—
Senator Spencer and
His Bride
(Correspondence of the Graphic*)*

DEADWOOD, DAKOTA, SEPTEMBER 27 – Deadwood seems very orderly just at present. To be sure, a couple of weeks ago, one of the owners of the Aurora Mine was shot and killed by some of the men at the Keets Mine. Their mines joined and each claimed the ore, and shooting seems the popular manner of settling disputes here. It is certainly a shorter and more decisive way than going to the law, and life does not seem of much value in this locality.

A Street Railroad

Some of our more enterprising citizens have just completed a survey of a narrow-gauge railroad for passengers and freight from Deadwood up the gulch to Gayville and Central City, with branches to the principle [sic] mines. The travel over this road amounts to over 1,500 persons a day, to say nothing of teams and wagons, and it is considered an excellent enterprise. It will prove a great benefit to Deadwood, for stamp mills can then be placed on Whitewood and Deadwood Gulches, where there is plenty of water. This has hitherto been impossible on account of the distance from the mines and the expense of hauling ore. Capitalists from New Bedford, Mass., are now on their way to the Hills with necessary funds for its construction, and think it an excellent investment.

"Road Agents" Again

Our road agents have robbed our stages with so much success, yet obtained so little of late, that they have tried their skill at larger game. They stopped the railroad train just beyond Cheyenne, and relieved the express car and passengers of over $70,000 besides watches, jewelry, etc. We were just congratulating ourselves that they had now gotten enough to enable them to retire from business, when last evening the news arrived that the stage from Deadwood to Sydney had been stopped, and not only the men robbed, but the women, too. They had heretofore left the women unsearched, and treated them with true Claude Duval chivalry and courtesy. It is supposed that the notorious James Boys are among this gang of road agents. It is said that one of them was seen and recognized on the road near Cheyenne River.

Two of this gang had a narrow escape from being captured a few days ago at Ft. Pierre, by which route they were evidently attempting to get out of the Hills. They were surprised and surrounded by a party of nine men, who called on them to surrender. They agreed, and as the men stepped forward to secure them they made a dash through the crowd, seized a gun from one man and through [sic] it in the river, jerked a revolver from another, and made for woods amid a shower of bullets, apparently unharmed. The whole band exhibits so much dash and disregard for their lives that it seems almost impossible to capture them.

A Youthful Hero

Apropos of bravery, what would mothers East think of the experience of this little boy of thirteen now in camp?

This little fellow started from Denver, Colorado, with his pony, and made the trip all the way to the Black Hills alone and on horse back, a distance of over 300 miles, principally through desolate plains or Indian country. He came in search of his father from whom he had not heard for some time. He found him "dead broke," as so many are here. The father took possession of the little fellow's pony, sold it, and soon spent the money, leaving the child destitute. He tried to get something to do, but was unable on account of his age. I found the little fellow sobbing bitterly, he had nothing to do and no pony on which to return home. The last

I heard of him, he had gone to herd horses on the Spearfish, a position of great danger, where one is constantly exposed to attacks from Indians, who await their chances to make a raid and carry off the stock. He is trying to earn enough money to buy back his pony, and return to Denver, before winter sets in. Poor little fellow! My heart aches for him, thrown on his own resources in this rough camp so early in life.

I have already spoken once or twice about the extreme profanity of the camp, but it is such a prominent and obtrusive feature that I cannot resist referring to it again. Before coming here, I had always been of the opinion that when people swore they [did so] out of temper, angry with each other and ready for a fight, but here one sees men swearing and laughing together in perfect friendliness and good fellowship. For instance, a man evidently going out of town just rode up and hastily accosted a friend on the sidewalk with, "By ______, give me a rifle." "By ______, I haven't any." "Well, give me a stick or a club or any ______ thing." "Here it is, ______ it. Now ain't you going to treat?" "Got sold that time, I haven't got a ______ cent. Goodbye," and with a laugh they both separated. This is merely a specimen of what one constantly hears throughout the Hills.

Senator Spencer's Wedding Tour

Bridal tours have been taken almost everywhere now-a-days, but it was reserved for Senator Spencer to inaugurate a wedding trip to the Black Hills. He and his beautiful wife arrived here a few days since, and Mrs. Spencer is perfectly enthusiastic about the Hills. The scenery, she says, is simply magnificent and equaled only by Switzerland. "People East cannot realize how grand it is from descriptions." The camp, she says, reminds her of a great fair; the bands playing music, the rush and bustle of the people, the display of the shops, and the white tents all around on the sides of the autumn tinted hills, all seem as if some great fete was in progress. The sluice mining in the street is a constant source of interest to her and all newcomers, many of whom have only a vague idea in regard to mining. We can only hope to keep the Senator and his wife with us a short time at present, as Congress meets soon, but all time not devoted to his duties in Washington will probably be spent here, as he is extensively in mining and mines in this locality.

"Wild Bill's" Head-board

The inscription on the headboard of "Wild Bill's" grave has become quite [a] curiosity to "Pilgrims" and many pay the already well-filled cemetery a visit before returning home for the purpose of copying it. For the benefit of your Eastern papers, I give it just as it appears on the board:

"Wild Bill"
J. B. Hickok,
Killed by the assassin
Jack M'Call
In
Deadwood, Black Hills,
August 24, 1876
Pard, we will
meet again
In the happy
Hunting Ground
To part no more.
Good bye.
"Colorado Charley"
C. H. Utter.

In the grave with him is buried all his guns, pistols, cartridges, belts, etc., that he died possessed of.

A Chance for An Enterprising Yankee

We are very much annoyed by the numerous rats and mice which infest our houses. How they come here is a mystery to us all. We are over two hundred miles from any town, the houses are all new, and the wood of which they are built was all hewn and sawed here. There isn't a cat in the Hills, and if some shrewd, enterprising Yankee would make a collection of some of your active midnight serenaders—some of whom you could well spare—and ship them to Deadwood, I am sure they would be in active demand, as they are much needed here.

The weather is becoming quite cold and everyone is preparing for winter. We may expect as intense cold here as they experience in St. Paul, Minnesota, as I believe we are about the same degree north. People are already plastering with mud the chinks in their log cabins, building chimneys and old fashioned fire places, and laying back logs for a long winter. The snow falls from one to four feet in depth, and the ground and water will be frozen most of the time; we may expect mining, prospecting, and milling to cease to a great extent until spring opens again. *Adrienne*[3]

Facts about the Black Hills
How Men Live, Move, and have their
Being in the New Elderado [sic]

A Plentitude of Gold and Hard Work—
Good Advice to Emigrants
(Correspondence to the Graphic*)*

DEADWOOD, OCTOBER 21 – Sunday here is scarcely observed in a religious way. To be sure, we have two churches, one Catholic and the other Congregational—but attendance is small. Business, as a general thing, still continues, the shops are open, the streets are thronged and gambling houses and liquor saloons do a more thriving business than on any other day. The variety theatres present an unusual bill of attractions on Sunday, and are crowded with appreciative audiences. The sidewalks can boast a greater number of drunken men, fights are frequent, and the name of the Lord is often heard, but only as mild form of swearing. Sunday is regarded in Deadwood more as a day of license and justification than a day of religious observance.

Frontier Expressions

Mining terms and "slang" combined with "swear words," are so much used here that it is difficult for a stranger to recognize and understand the language. To say that someone has "sand" means that he has pluck or courage. If anyone improves on acquaintance he "pans out well;" if his finances are at their lowest ebb he is "Down to bedrock." If anyone is skillful at anything he is a "sharp." When a man is truthful, he "carries a little hatchet right along with him." To investigate anything is to "prospect it," an enterprising and wide-awake man is "rustler." When a man dies "he passes in his checks," or "goes up the flume." The highest praise one can give is to say "he is a white man, yes sir." The word sir is never omitted out here, and plays an important part in the conversation. Yes or no do not sound half as emphatic without that little word sir, and it is sometimes made to sound very aggressive, as "what do you mean, sir;" "______ you, sir;" "take that, sir," followed by a blow. "Howdy" is the invariable salutation, followed up by the question, "what do you know?" One hears constantly of the "Boss house," the "boss mine," the "boss dinner or feed." A newcomer is a "tenderfoot," or "pilgrim," a settler is a "stranger," when a man is bald, "his head is above the timberline;" if a man is well informed and intelligent, "he has heap of savey [savvy]," and so on *ad infinitum*.

Inquiries in Regard to the Hills

Letter[s] reach us everyday containing inquiries in regards to the Hills and asking in substance the following questions, the answers to which may be interesting to your readers:

Which is the best season of the year to take a trip to the Black Hills?

What is the best route there from the East?

What outfit is required?

Is there gulch mining only, or is the gold embedded in quartz?

Are all the good mines discovered and taken up, or is there still a chance to discover and locate?

If one does not succeed in finding a good claim, can other employment be obtained, and at what rates?

Spring is decidedly the most favorable season of the year to come to the Black Hills, and April and May are the best months. In the winter all mining is more or less stopped, and winter begins early and lasts late; snow falls from one to four feet deep; the ground and water is, of course, frozen, and gulch claims can hardly be worked at all.

The best and most direct route here is from St. Louis to Omaha, from there to Cheyenne and from Cheyenne by stage to Deadwood. The stage journey is accomplished in fifty-four to sixty hours, and but twenty-five pounds of baggage is allowed each person.

No particular outfit is required; everything necessary can be bought here about as cheap as they could be brought in. Of course, a rifle, a revolver, a pair of blankets and a bottle of whiskey are considered necessary to every traveler, and hardly need be suggested. Board here is $16 a week, and table board is $10.

Plenty of Gold

That gold exists in the Black Hills, and in great quantities, is beyond doubt, the proof of which is the fact that the banks have shipped out over $250,000 in gold per month, and for the months of August and September the shipments reached over $400,000 each month. The gold belt extends over a distance of sixty miles in length by forty in width, and there is an excellent silver district, eight miles long by two miles wide. Excellent mines have been discovered all over this region, and new ones are being discovered daily. The ore is free milling ore and the gold easily saved. It assays all the way from nothing to about $15.00. There are more than forty stamp mills now in camp, working day and night, and more are constantly arriving. When a good lode is discovered there is no difficulty getting a stamp mill located on it, which will extract the gold for a moderate profit per ton. The camp is pronounced by every one the most wonderful one of its age ever seen.

It is useless for more men destitute of money to emigrate to the Hills. Mining is uncertain; they may or may not strike something that will pay, and in the meantime they must live, and living here is expensive. Thousands came to the Hills last spring without a cent, expecting to pick up nuggets in the streets. They were not acquainted with the first principles of mining or prospecting, couldn't tell quartz from Granite, and didn't have time to learn. Those who could raise money enough to leave have done so, and the others still remain, doing whatever they can to keep themselves from starving.

Employment is difficult to obtain here. Every trade and occupation is crowded. There are however, excellent opportunities to make good investments; and this is the class of men we need now—men to assist by their capital to develop the country.

The Black Hills as a Farming Country

Practical farming would doubtless pay well here, and all crops raised could be disposed of to excellent advantage. At the present all most everything we consume in the way [of] vegetables, grain, and etc., has to be brought in from Cheyenne—a distance of nearly 300 miles—and commands large prices. Farming has been tried here this season, but only to a limited extent, and more as an experiment, but with such good success that next year we may in all probability expect our market will be supplied with home produce.

In conclusion, I would say that the life of a miner or prospector is not one to covet, and would advise anyone who is making a decent livelihood in the East not to give it up for the precarious and uncomfortable life of a seeker of gold in the Black Hills. The miners as a general thing live near their claims, in canvas tents or small one roomed log cabins, the chinks and roofs plastered with mud. Three or four live together and "batch," as they term it here—that is, do their own work, cooking and washing too, if their colored ever do get washed. Such luxuries as sheets and pillow are unknown among them. Their beds consist of a pair of colored blankets on a straw ticking and a boot for a pillow. Their food consists principally of bacon and bread. Sickness is very prevalent among them, and typhoid, or mountain fever, as it is known here, carries off many. The life and companionship is very demoralizing if one can judge by the profanity, foulness, and drunkenness which exists among them.

I suppose there will be still greater excitement about the Hills in the spring, for the mines are improving. California capitalists are here investing in mines. Two of the best, the "Golden Terra" and the "Homestake" are already in their hands, and Black Hills mines will soon figure on the California Stock Exchange. Professor Jenin has been sent here by the California Stock Board to investigate and negotiate for the purchase of mines, and is enthusiastic about them. Of course all of this makes a great deal of business and the people here are building large sized air-castles. *Adrienne*[4]

Adrienne Webster Davis' fifth article from her home in Deadwood, Dakota Territory, to the *New York Daily Graphic.*

Prospects in the Black Hills

Signs of the Times That Show the March of Civilization

Stock Speculators from California and New York Buying up the Mines

(Correspondence to the Graphic*)*

DEADWOOD, D.T., FEBRUARY 20 – It is wonderful—the rapid growth of Deadwood. One can scarcely realize that it is the same city that stood here a year ago, for nearly all its picturesque roughness has disappeared. We now have fine hotels, a theatre, large shops, numerous banks, some handsome residences, with plate glass and bow windows, and school houses are being built, we take fashion magazines, order our clothes from New York, pay calls with visiting cards, and sometimes even in a carriage. The usual bed in the corner of the sitting room or parlor is rapidly being replaced by the piano. One or two dinner parties have been given, and several evening parties attempted. You can easily see from all this that we are rapidly becoming civilized, and yet the town is barely two years old.

Outside the city the improvement is still more marked. In Gayville, Central, and Lead City, the pounding of hundreds of stamps constantly in operation, the whir of the machinery of the mills and the shriek of the steam whistles, remind one of the busiest of our Eastern manufacturing towns.

The advent of Californians has given a wonderful impetus to the development of the Black Hills. Numerous companies have been organized in California, with capital ranging from $5,000,000 to $12,000,000 for the purchase of Black Hills mining property. Each company has sent a representative here, empowered to purchase all mines that on investigation justify representation. Jim Keene, Mark McDonald, Flood & O'Brien, George Hearst, and other prominent California stock brokers, have their experts here, and when they happen to bid against each other the game grows exciting. The mines already purchased by them are the Father de Smet for

$400,000, the Homestake for $70,000, and had they not bonded it for that amount, they could have, one week after obtained $350,000 for the same property. One thousand feet of the Golden Terra sold for $80,000 to one party, and five hundred feet to another for $90,000. The Old Abe brought $42,500, the Giant $40,000, and others of less importance sold for smaller sums. Negotiations are still pending for the Caledonia and Homestake No. 2, and others equally good remain in the hands of the original owners. These mines have an ore body varying from 20 feet in width to 133[.] ½ solid ore. This last immense ore body exists in the Father De Smet mine. Some of these mines are already paying dividends, and all are, or soon will be, quoted in the San Francisco stock market.

The difference between the California and Eastern capitalists is very marked indeed. The Californian arrives and begins sampling a mine the very next day. He measures the amount of ore in site, finds out how much it assays per ton and pays cash down the day after. Our Eastern friend takes a couple of weeks looking at a mine, suspects a fraud or swindle in everything, tries to bargain and beat down the price, and when he finally decides it is all right and concludes to take it, he finds the ground cut from beneath his feet by the more enterprising Californian.

It will not be long before California owns all or the greater part of Black Hills property. A company has been organized, and have purchased the right of way and water privilege, and are about building a flume for carrying lumber and supplying the mills and the city with good water. This will prove a good and paying enterprise, as many mills are often forced to "shut down" on account of lack of water. It will also be much appreciated in Deadwood, as water in town at present is much contaminated by mineral and vegetable matter on account of mining, and causes much illness.

Typhoid or "mountain fever" has prevailed here extensively and is a terrible disease. It lasts from three to eight weeks, accompanied by great suffering and delirium, and unless the patient has an excellent constitution is likely to prove fatal. Having it once does not prevent one from having it again, or as many times as the system is prepared for it. The proprietor of the Welch is a gentleman of fine appearance and considerable wealth, and it has been a continual wonder to his many friends why he never married. It seems he was some years ago engaged to a charming girl in the East, and a short time before the wedding day they had some misunderstanding and parted. She, in a fit of pique, married another. After a few years she became a widow, and he hearing of this opened correspondence and renewed his suit, which resulted in her joining him here and their marriage. Their happiness was of short duration, however, for they had only been married two days before she fell victim to this terrible mountain fever, and three weeks after her wedding day, her funeral took place, attended by nearly all Deadwood as sympathizing mourners.

The Chinese New Year begins on the 1st of February, and is an interesting institution. A few days previous to that date my Chinese laundryman, "Wik," informed me that he "no washee, no iron this week," he "eat Chicken and make joss allee time." Their inability to pronounce the letter "r" makes strange havoc with our language. On the arrival of the day he presented me with some curious confectionary and Chinese date nuts, also several boxes of red and white paint "to make face and lips pletty," and invited me to call. I went, and found a wonderful picture of a Joss or Chinese God, with numerous arms and legs, hung on the wall, and beneath it a kind of altar, covered with curious dishes of Chinese cake, pastry, confectionary and nuts, and scraps of paper with printed Chinese prayers. My host was arrayed in a gorgeous costume of blue quilted silk, without sleeves and several yards of freshly braided queue. He said "Howdy," and invited us to be seated and treated us to the Chinese food on the alter [sic]. I tasted in fear and trembling, for although some of it was very good, yet I did not know what I might be eating. It might be a conserve of mice or something equally delicate for all I knew. So I ate daintily and he made a package of what was left, which I put into the fire on my return home. In the evening the Chinese quarter of the city was illuminated by fireworks, crackers, rockets, and roman candles. The next day was spent in fasting and distribution of the paper prayers, and all was over till next year.

The camp never was so prosperous. It has been pronounced by numerous visitors here as the richest and most wonderful mining country in the United States, excepting for Virginia City, Nevada, and in time may even rival that. Prospecting goes on constantly, an army of them are attacking the Hills in all directions, and new locations are made daily; Indians and Road Agents, all things of the past. The stage route is perfectly safe, and even at this season of the year full coach loads are constantly arriving. The new arrivals are principally men of capital and enterprise, and from indications we may expect a crowd of all classes and conditions this summer. A railroad into the Hills will be begun this summer, and other enterprises are contemplated. Coal has been discovered in great quantities a short distance from town. An analysis of the coal proves it to be something in between a bituminous and an anthracite—a sort of brown coal. The coal fields are being surveyed and taken up, and next year we may expect glowing coal fires instead of always—to—be—replenished fires of pine wood.

I must renew my advice to those who anticipate making a trip to the Black Hills. There is hardly anything for men to do except prospecting and they may or may not be successful in that. Old miners from Nevada, Montana, California, and Colorado are here in great numbers—men who are as familiar with gold bearing quartz, croppings, and indications as they are with the alphabet, men accustomed to the hard life and the scant living as a miner. They occasionally strike something, make a sale, spend the money, and start again. The "tenderfoot" who comes here expecting to pick up nuggets on the road, or strike at the first blow of the pick, and who cannot tell quartz from granite, had better stay home. After all, the men who manipulate the miners, are those who make the money, not the miners. Men who have some capital, good mill men, and men with good trades have their value in every community. Living, provisions, clothes, tools, everything, in fact is high here, and will continue to be as long as everything has to be hauled by ox or mule teams from Cheyenne at a cost of 5 to 8 cents per pound freight. In conclusion I must say—don't leave a certainty for an uncertainty, no matter how glittering it appears in the distance. *Adrienne*[5]

Adrienne Davis's time in Deadwood was to be sadly cut short. See the following chapter about her husband Chambers C. Davis—and their respective fates.

CHAPTER FOUR

CHAMBERS DAVIS: THE BRIEF LIFE OF DEADWOOD'S FIRST ASSAYER

He was the kind of "up-and-comer" that new western towns wanted, a civic-minded young businessman providing an essential service and fully involved in social and political life, but Chambers Davis's promise did not bloom for long.

In 1874, the cry of "Gold in the Black Hills" brought a cross-section of Americans to their feet after Custer confirmed that the metal could be plucked from the streams. The mind's eye often only focuses on the romance and drama of the mining environment: men panning in the streams for gold, prospectors scrutinizing every crevice and rock in remote gulches and on mountaintops. But in reality a gold rush mobilizes a plethora of

CHAMBERS C. DAVIS' ASSAY OFFICE AND METTALLURGICAL WORKS.

Our cut, although comparatively inexpressive of what is within the building it represents, portrays one of the most complete, valuable and popular establishments in the West—the assay office and metallurgical works of Chambers C. Davis, Esq., Deadwood. Every separate branch of the business is allotted a separate apartment, and the latest and most approved machinery and appliances for the testing of ore and refining of bullion, can be seen within.

It is a matter more of justice and valuable information to mining operators, than a compliment to the gentleman named when the editor calls the attention of the mining public and others desiring assays of mineral bearing rock, to the very complete and extensive assay office and mineral testing establishment of Mr. Chambers C. Davis, located at the head of Main street, Deadwood. We need scarcely say more of Mr. Davis' thorough ability in his calling than that he learned his profession at the Philadelphia Mint under Mr Eckfeldt, and on the establishment of the Denver Mint was placed in charge of the Assay Department. He was afterward the Melter and Refiner, in fact, had charge of the executive department. He was for years the Chief Assayer of the great Comstock mines, being for a long time in the special employment of the Bonanza kings—Flood, O'Brien, Mackey and Fair—his position one of marked importance, and his assays stamping the value of millions; but it will better convey the purpose of our information to say that Mr. Davis' assay certificates are ones that bear weight here among our mining and mill operators. Parties from a distance may thoroughly rely upon tests made, and that all business entrusted to his hands will be given faithful attention. Letters should be addressed: "Chambers C. Davis, Assayer, Deadwood, D. T."

Mining Dictionary.

Under this head a few of the mining terms most frequently used are correctly defined to more readily assist comprehension in perusing mining reports.

Amalgam—Bullion and quicksilver, before separation.

Adit—A cut across or into a mine.

Bed-rock The rock, slate or clay formation underlying the pay dirt; in quartz, that underlying an ore deposit.

Breasting ore—Taking ore from the face of a mine.

Blind Lode—A mine that shows no croppings on the surface.

Bastard Quartz—A species of quartzite or quartz containing no valuable mineral.

Croppings—The reef of quartz rock that appears on the surface, indicating the presence of a fissure.

Chute—An incline from an upper tunnel or level to a lower one, through which to slide ore.

Cap rock—The formation overlying the pay-dirt, or ore.

Drift—A short tunnel run from the main tunnel or shaft. In placer mining a tunnel run on bed-rock through which to work the pay-gravel in deep diggings.

Dump—The place where ore is put after being taken from the mine.

Face—The extreme end of a tunnel, drift or excavation where work is prosecuted.

Foot wall—In defined fissure quartz veins, the lower rock formation dividing the ore from the country rock.

Float rock—Portions of the main lode separated from it and thrown at a distance by volcanic action or the elements. Mines are found by tracing the "float"

The Black Hills News *lauded Davis's experience as an assayer for the Philadelphia and Denver Mints.*

skills, talents, and educational backgrounds, many of which are invisible and unsung, but are as crucial as the miners' abilities. This is the story of such a man, Deadwood's first assayer.

Chambers C. Davis arrived in Deadwood toward the end of April 1877. On his arrival, he announced that he was the representative of the San Francisco banking house Flood and O'Brine, with a standing letter of credit for $100,000. He also brought his intention to make Deadwood an enduring community that he could grow with.

Davis was born in Pennsylvania, and worked at his father's inn until the outbreak of the Civil War. In September 1861, Davis enlisted into the 8th Pennsylvania Cavalry as a bugler. By August 1863, when he was transferred to the reserve, he had been cited for Distinguished Service and had attained the rank of sergeant. Following his discharge, twenty-two-year-old Davis moved to Denver where he and a partner, Rodney Curtis, operated a wholesale/retail grocery store on the corner of Larimer and F Streets, offering fancy and staple groceries, along with coal, lumber, and hardware, which they advertised continuously in the *Rocky Mountain News* during 1865 and 1866. The partners also purchased local produce in October 1865, advertising their business to farmers to save the agriculture men from traveling house to house hawking their vegetables. Another ad that December let customers know they could drop a grocery basket and their order at the store in the morning on the way to work, and the store would deliver the purchases to their homes.

In May 1868, President Andrew Johnson nominated Davis and partner Curtis to take over positions at the Denver Mint. By June 26, this had been approved unanimously by the U.S. Senate, and Davis became the head smelter and refiner at the U.S. Mint.

While at the Mint, Davis met and, in May 1874 at the Manitou Hot Springs Hotel, married Miss Adrienne Webster. Standing four inches above five feet, the bride was blessed with a fair complexion, red hair, and blue eyes. In a nice article after the wedding, the *Denver Daily Times* related that Davis wished to keep it a tastefully quiet affair, but due to Davis's popularity, he had problems containing the event. His bride was said to be one of the brightest and most fascinating ladies in the ranks of Colorado newcomers.[1] Immediately following the wedding, the couple departed on honeymoon to New York.

After gaining seven years of experience working at the Denver mint, Davis resigned from the mint and took the job as assayer for the Consolidated Virginia and California Mining Company of Virginia City, Nevada, in its Deadwood facility.[2]

One of the first things that Davis set out to do when he arrived in

Davis's two-story assay office in Deadwood is seen here just below and right of center, with his business sign, "CHAMBERS C DAVIS ASSAYER," atop the roof.

Deadwood was locate a satisfactory mill site in the Bear Butte Mining District, near Galena, for his employer Flood and O'Brien. It took him just several weeks to accomplish this, and then he opened his own assay office at the head of Main Street in Deadwood.

One of the primary jobs of an assayer is to determine the percentage of metals contained in a given sample of ore. Based on the assayer's report and his reputation in the field, a mine may be valued for sale or investment purposes. The assay report will also determine how much can be spent processing the ore profitably. In May 1877, one of Davis's earliest assays was done on ore from the Silver Chief Mine, and showed a value of $218.70 per ton in silver.

During the same period of time, Davis was also working on the placer gold dust from various claims for different banks throughout the city, smelting the metal samples at his metallurgical works and casting them into bars. His metallurgical works was described in a May 26, 1877, *Black Hills Times* article: "His laboratory is supplied with three furnaces made of heavy shell iron, lined with imported firebrick. One is used for melting gold dust, another for crucible assays of ore. In the rear of the office and laboratory is a two-stamp mill, run by a portable steam engine of eight horse power."[3]

In his arsenal, Davis also had a rock crusher, which made the news in June 1877 when he shipped it to Bear Butte Mining district to sample ore that he was intending to purchase. Early the following month, Davis started shipping ore from the Yellow Jacket mine to the smelting works in St. Louis, Missouri.[4]

It must have been obvious to the entire town that Chambers C. Davis was not a man to sit on his hands and wait for the gold to find him, but above all that he was a man who believed in "community." He did his duties as a grand juror, was on the executive committee to form a new territory from the Black Hills—to be called Lincoln Territory—and by September 1877 he had proposed a plan to build a narrow-gauge railway from upper Sherman Street to Central City. William Beard and H. P. Bennet supported Davis in this plan.

Davis started rebuilding his business structures in February 1878. The *Times* said that the new structures were the result of Davis's "rapidly augmenting business." His new building was described as being thirty by thirty-two feet on the ground, two stories tall, with a sixteen- by twenty-foot rear addition. The main structure was to be divided into an office, library specimen room, and private apartments. The rear addition would be used for smelting purposes. "In fact, the establishment will be equal in appointment to the best assay works on the Pacific coast. Everything necessary for the extraction of the precious metals from virgin rock has been procured by Mr. Davis for his new institution. This is what we call enterprise."[5]

In a separate article, the paper noted that Davis was also installing hot and cold running-water bath arrangements in his new building, the first of its kind in a private structure in the Black Hills.

During construction, Davis and Adrienne were living at the Wentworth House hotel when it was announced that she had become seriously ill. On May 1, 1878, Dr. Bevens of Deadwood was called for consultation, and pronounced her to be in very serious condition. But on the 8th, the *Times* informed the public that Mrs. Davis was recovering rapidly.

About the time of his wife's illness, Chambers Davis became convinced that between forty and fifty percent of the gold ore going through the stamp mill process in the Black Hills was being lost down the mill's tail-

An advertisement for his assay business mentions the melting process that eventually led to Davis's demise. This ad ran in the May 8, 1877, edition of the Black Hills Daily Times.

race. The tailrace is part of a millrace below the stamps and amalgamation tables, through which the spent water flows to carry away mine tailings and refuse. Davis's conviction was so firm that he sent 1,000 pounds of mill tailings to Philadelphia, at his own expense, to be treated with a new extraction process.

By May 20, Adrienne Davis had recovered enough strength that she was able to move from Wentworth House to the family's new residence at the head of Main Street. Only two weeks later, on June 3, in a tragic turn of health, Adrienne died in her new home. Chambers Davis, apparently unable to let his wife go, buried her behind the building on a point of land at the head of Centennial Avenue.

One week later, the *Times* ran this brief note: "The lonely grave of Mrs. C. C. Davis, on the point at the head of Centennial Avenue, was numerously visited by friends on Sunday afternoon who literally bedecked it with wild flowers."[6] The Lawrence County death record gave Adrienne's age as thirty-three. Described by the *Times* as a most beautiful and gifted lady, she had written letters to the *New York Graphic* recounting life in Deadwood and other mining fronts, which were often republished nationally.

In June, the *Black Hills Daily Times* reprinted an article from the *New York Graphic*, written in tribute to Adrienne. A very similar article was also published by the *Denver Daily Tribune*, which spoke of her contributions to the *New York Graphic* and her social standing in the Denver community.

Soon after the death of his wife, Davis began accumulating real estate. First he bought the Buffalo Corral property, and then Frenchy the Bottle Fiend's "bottle ranch" on City Creek. These properties adjoined land he already owned at the head of Main Street. A month after Adrienne died, Davis purchased a 600-ounce gold scale, the largest in the Black Hills, and he appeared to be digging in his heels to stay with Deadwood for the long haul. He was working hard and now, alone, so very little social news was heard of Davis for the rest of the year. Then, in December, he was injured in a crucible explosion that damaged one of his eyes.

Following that accident, the newspapers were again silent when it came to news of Davis until the next spring, when the *Times* followed a series of events that would have made Preacher Smith turn over in his grave. Davis had been busy melting a gold bar. The bar also had in it naturally occurring impurities such as antimony. To remove it, Davis boiled the bar in a bath of potassium cyanide and nitric acid. The fumes of this most deadly combination were supposed to escape up the flue of his furnace, but instead went up Davis's nose. It was reported that he was "quite out of his head for some hours afterward. All appeared well the next morning, except Davis was "suffering some inconvenience from excessive drooling."[7]

Four days later, the *Black Hills Pioneer* announced that Davis's doctors had pronounced him insane. The article continued, "Mr. Davis has been so intimately known to most of our people that their condolence will be spontaneous and heartfelt. He is a man that we cannot afford to lose, as his eminent skill as a metallurgist was unequalled here or anywhere, and his opinion on minerals had become law in this country."[8]

Naturally, the competing *Times* countered this by consulting the physician attending Davis, Dr. McKown. The doctor told the *Times* that the article in the *Pioneer* had appeared without his knowledge or consent, and that there was no indication that Davis's present condition was permanent.

The next event was amazing: the Reverend Atwood united Davis with Miss M. Alice Sahler in marriage on April 14, just seven days after the accident. The wedding announcement also stated that Davis was up and about and recovering nicely from his previous accident.

But later that week, the *Times* ran a single sentence that read: "C. C. Davis is not improving." A few days later, it announced that Davis was suffering from "softening of the brain" and was unlikely to recover. The next day Davis slipped into a coma and "Grim Death is tugging away at the knot of his life and is liable to untie it at any moment."[9]

Chambers C. Davis died in the afternoon of April 24, 1879, just seventeen days after the accident and ten days after his second wedding. The question that begs being asked a century and a quarter later is: If Davis's mental state was something less than stable, how could the marriage have been allowed to happen? Was this a nineteenth century method of appointing him a guardian? And just who was M. Alice Sahler?

Born in Nebraska in 1860, Alice was nineteen years old at the time of her marriage to Davis, who was exactly twice her age. Less than a year previously, Alice had been named a "Deadwood Beauty," riding in the "car of state" as the Goddess of Liberty for the Fourth of July parade. If the newspaper accounts were correct, one gets a mental picture of a beautiful young bride in white, standing next to an older man who is drooling, his eyes rolling around in his head like so many marbles.

The imagination flies: Was Alice his housekeeper? His lover, who had been waiting in the wings for Chambers to end his traditional year of mourning? Was Chambers in any condition to consummate a marriage?

If perhaps the marriage was a scam designed to capture a share of the Davis fortune, Alice was out of luck. Davis's probate painted the portrait of an energetic man who believed in what he was doing enough to mortgage everything he owned to make it happen and, in the end, the grieving widow was forced into court to save the very home she lived in.

The probate records also give an intimate glimpse into the life of Chambers Davis and his first wife, Adrienne. It lists items such as pearl and gold cufflinks, and silver napkin rings monogrammed with "Chambers" and "Adrienne." It also told of family photographs showing Chambers, Adrienne, and a previously unknown infant daughter, along with a suitcase of children's clothing.

By 1881, Adrienne's body was moved from her original grave to the plot next to Chambers' at Mount Moriah Cemetery. Chambers had received a fitting Masonic funeral, but no marker. In August 1895, Adrienne's father arrived in Deadwood to visit her grave. Upon receiving directions from Henry Robinson, the undertaker, he had no problem finding where Adrienne and Chambers were buried. He made arrangements with Robinson to have the grounds around the grave improved and a temporary wooden headboard put up. A while later, Mr. Webster ordered the stone monument seen today at the grave site. It does not appear that at the time of his death there had been enough left of the Chambers Davis estate for even a wooden headboard.

In February of 1882, a brief article ran in the *Black Hills Daily Times* announcing the marriage of the widow of Chambers C. Davis in Omaha. Alice had moved there with her parents, where she had met a Mr. Fleming, chief clerk for a large Omaha drug company. One portion of the wedding announcement sounded ironically identical to Adrienne Davis' obituary: "Mrs. Davis is a highly accomplished, intellectual and estimable young lady, and has an extensive circle of friends and admirers who join the [Omaha] *Bee* in hearty congratulations and well wishes for the future happiness of the bridegroom and bride." No indication was given as to the physical or mental condition of the new groom.[10]

CHAPTER FIVE

CON STAPLETON: DEADWOOD'S FIRST MARSHAL

Four years after this young Irishman arrived in the States, he became Deadwood's first town marshal—finding himself embroiled in a messy, dangerous manhunt. Stapleton was elected in Deadwood's very first balloting, along with Mayor Farnum, whose story is told elsewhere in this book.

Born in 1848, Con Stapleton first set foot on American soil on May 17, 1872, in New York City. He had departed Ireland from Queenstown and made the journey berthed in the steerage section of the sailing steamer *Manhattan*.

The *Manhattan* was a large two-masted steamer that carried cargo and immigrants from Europe to the United States. On the voyage that brought Con Stapleton to the United States, she was carrying more than 600 passengers, most of whom were traveling third class.

From New York, Stapleton traveled to Montana, where, in July 1874, he was noted in several editions of Helena's *Daily Independent* as running for constable in the Helena Precinct of Lewis and Clark County.

He first appears in Deadwood news in the *Black Hills Pioneer* when he was elected town marshal as part of the initial quasi-legal city government in September 1876[1]. On September 25, he was in the news again when John Manning and others of the community advertised the formation of the Democrats of Lawrence County. Stapleton was noted to be one of the newly elected delegates to a proposed party convention that would occur on September 29.

Marshal Stapleton had his first real taste of duty when he received information and a photograph of a man who was wanted in Marion County, Iowa. The man, Horry Williams, had been convicted of murder.

The judge asked him, after he was sentenced to twenty years imprisonment, if he had anything to say. His reply was short and to the point, "You may pass sentence on me, but I will never serve the term." Later, as the local sheriff was transporting him to Iowa's state penitentiary, Williams overcame the officer and beat him to a "state of insensibility." He then made his escape, and reportedly had been seen in Deadwood.

On March 24 the following year, Stapleton solicited the assistance of Captain Hardwick and hit the trail in search of the desperado. They first traveled to Elk Creek, where they found that they were on the right trail, but a day and a half late. They spent the night at Elk Creek and by 6 A.M. were back in hard pursuit. They rode to Battle River, and followed its course to Iron Creek.

Here they encountered a cabin whose residents confirmed that the man they were looking for had been staying there but was presently out hunting. Stapleton and Hardwick decided to wait at the cabin for Williams' return. At just about 5 P.M., the cabin door opened and they stood staring into the face of Horry Williams. Williams put away his gun at the request of his host, Dr. Woods, and sat down to dinner. While he was eating and engaged in conversation, the marshal and the captain arrested him. Williams was transported back to Deadwood without incident, and the authorities in Iowa were notified. Captain Hardwick then returned Williams to Iowa and prison.

The Shooting of David Lunt

A bunch of Stapleton's friends were sitting around having drinks and shooting the breeze at Al Chapman's Saloon, which was located right next to the Senate Saloon, on the cold winter evening of January 14, 1877. Included in the group were Con Stapleton and David Lunt. Lunt was a very well-liked man around town, with a reputation of being fair and genial. The conversation was good, the saloon was warm, and drinks were cheap.

All of a sudden the saloon door burst open. A man named Tom Smith came in and drew his revolver. Smith stated that if anyone moved he would shoot him. He approached the group that included Lunt, leveled his revolver and continued shouting threats. At this point, Stapleton grabbed Smith and was attempting to disarm him when the revolver went off. The ball narrowly missed Stapleton's head, continued on and struck David Lunt in the forehead.

Smith was arrested and brought to trial over the incident, but it appears that the only charge they could get him on at the time was discharging a firearm at a town marshal. In court, the fact that David Lunt was also shot during the fracas did not seem to enter into the verdict. Tom Smith was taken off to Yankton for a real trial, which also did not consider the fact that Lunt was shot, and by March of the same year Smith could be found walking the streets of San Francisco.

But what about Lunt? Well of course everyone thought that he was going to die, and soon, but instead he got up and started to do the same things he had been doing before he was shot. He actually seemed like his old self, even though a bullet had passed completely through his skull, until March 22, when he began complaining of an extremely bad headache. Mr. and Mrs. Morgan, friends who owned the Centennial Hotel, took him in and tried to nurse him back to health, but he kept sinking lower and that night, at about 10:45, he died.

Drs. Bevan and Babcock conducted a post-mortem the following morning. Their findings were that the bullet had passed through Lunt's head, and in the process the bullet had carried an inch-and-half-long bone fragment deep into his brain. The bone fragment caused a large abscess to form, and the right hemisphere of the brain began to fill with fluid. Now the determination was made that Smith had committed murder, and so

Sheriff Seth Bullock sent a telegram to ascertain Smith's whereabouts and to issue a warrant for his arrest. Smith was arrested in San Francisco and sent back to Yankton for trial. Amazingly, David Lunt had lived for sixty-seven days with a bullet hole through his skull and brain.

The Drawbacks of Not Having a Jail

As usual, most mining camp calamities happened at night and in a saloon, and such was the case of the shooting of Harry Varnes. Thirteen days after the tragedy of David Lunt's shooting, Varnes was shot and killed at Hanley's Gayville saloon. The event started over what had been a friendly Saturday evening card game on January 27, 1877.

At the end of the game, one of the players, a blacksmith named Hartgrove, was angered over the outcome. Hartgrove made several statements that enraged Varnes. Varnes then stood up, raising his chair over his head so as to hit Hartgrove with it. The chair never fell, because the saloon's proprietor restrained Varnes. Simultaneously Hartgrove drew his revolver, but was prevented from firing it by several of Varnes' friends. A short time elapsed and the crisis appeared to have ended, and then Hartgrove stalked out of the saloon, but remained on the walk outside the door. Varnes called out to Hartgrove, asking him to come back in and have a drink, but Hartgrove declined.

Between 10 and 11 P.M., Hartgrove kicked open the door to the saloon as he stood outside. The previous argument was revived, and Hartgrove again drew his revolver and shot at Varnes through the door. With Varnes dying on the saloon floor, Hartgrove vanished into the night.

The next morning, at about 6 A.M., Hartgrove woke up Marshal Stapleton at his rooms in Deadwood and explained what had happened the previous night, stating that he wished to give himself up. Stapleton replied, "All right; but you know we have no jail here, so you must stop for the present where you are." Hartgrove sat down and began waiting. Soon he started complaining of being pretty cold, so Stapleton told him to fire up the stove downstairs, and that he would be along when he was ready. Hartgrove warmed himself by the fire until about 9 A.M., when Stapleton came downstairs and joined him. At that time Hartgrove asked Marshal Stapleton if he could go consult with his lawyers, who had offices on the second floor of the same building. Somewhere between the stove and the lawyer's office, Hartgrove decided that he had inconvenienced Deadwood and its marshal long enough and, to quote the *Pioneer*, "That was the last seen of the perpetrator of this dread deed, and no doubt long ere this he is out of the reach of law or justice."

On November 7, 1877, Con Stapleton's job as marshal was finished. The office of city marshal ceased to exist and its duties taken were over by the sheriff of Lawrence County. Stapleton stayed in the Deadwood area until the next year. He was featured several times at the Gem Theatre, once in a sparring match, another time in a wrestling contest, and the last time as the referee for another wrestling match. After February of 1877, Stapleton drifted south to Denver, where it was reported that he died on September 10, 1879. He would have been about thirty-one years old.

CHAPTER SIX

SARAH ANN ERB: MADAME OF THE BULLDOG RANCHES

Messy and vindictive divorces, with plenty of legal tomfoolery demanding far too much attention from the justice system, are certainly not a modern invention, as the ongoing saga of Sarah Ann and John Joseph Erb reveals.

Divorce, during the initial decade of the gold rush, was a most newsworthy item in the northern hills. The earliest published record of such an event was in the *Black Hills Daily Times* on November 12, 1877, when Susan Boyd divorced her husband, J. D.[1] Perhaps the most common reason for divorce was the prolonged absence of the husband. Rosa Deamond waited two years before seeking a July 1879 divorce from her husband, who had wandered off to find riches.[2] The first published record of alimony in the Black Hills appears to have been the monies awarded in January of 1880, when as part of her decree a Mrs. Ward asked to be paid $4 a week.[3] For comparison, a hotel room in the hot mining mecca of Rochford then was going for $2.50 a day.[4]

There seemed to have been some mysterious laws at the time, where a person could get a partial divorce. After obtaining a partial divorce, you were prohibited by law from getting married again.[5] It was exactly this sort of legal tomfoolery that initiated Madame Bulldog's public life.

In the history of the Deadwood area are several spots on the map called "Bulldog." There is a ranch on the Rochford Road called the Bulldog Ranch. Near Fort Meade National Cemetery are Bulldog Road, Bulldog Creek, and Bulldog Gulch. This was also the location of the New Bulldog Ranch. The Erb family, or more correctly, John Joseph Erb, first appeared in September 1878 newspapers when he decided to purchase a tidy ranch out on the Rochford Road.[6] While the ranch was not a regular stage stop, it was on the Rochford Road, and it frequently had visitors. Bullwhackers, muleskinners, and other hungry and thirsty travelers often enjoyed the hospitality of the ranch during that first year. The madame of the house ran a small saloon and was known to rustle up a generous plateful of grub when asked. Mrs. Erb, or Sarah Ann, was also known as Madame Bulldog because she kept two dogs tethered outside to make sure the casual passerby did not abscond with one of her most precious commodities, the chickens. There is no way of knowing what wedge was driven between Sarah Ann and Joe, but there were strong hints that the problem was another, younger man.

Other than the initial purchase of the ranch, Deadwood reporters had made no comment about the Bulldog Ranch or its owners over the next year. Then suddenly a flurry of stories erupted in the first week of August 1879 when it was noted that "Madam Erb, of Bulldog Ranch" was in town seeking a separation from her husband. Her husband, John Joseph, was more than a little concerned about the situation and had taken to following her about town, but on that first Sunday of August he may have been just a little too close. The madame had stepped into a pawnshop, and Joe, curious about what items might be financing his legal woes, poked his head in the door. At this point things happened fast; either Sarah Ann was showing the pawn broker a pistol or she was the fastest draw in the Midwest. She whipped around and flashed a gun in Joe's startled face. The published version of Joe's escape was that he "cut out like quarter horse."

At this point, the local press must have stampeded down to the local saloons to find out what was really happening with the lovely Sarah Ann, and a low-down they must have received, for the next day they published the grist that makes their mill turn. The *Daily Times* began its examination of the situation by informing the public that Sarah Ann had been "obliged to pack revolvers around in every pocket to keep her old man in a proper state of intimidation, but he had stolen marches on her."[7]

The problem between Joe and Sarah Ann had been brewing for some time, and the Sunday before, that would be August 3, while Sarah Ann was in the city, Joe started pulling shenanigans. It seems that he loaded up several teams with the household furniture, and then rounded up the stock and lit out for Deadwood. On the way, Joe dropped the livestock and some of the furniture off at Ten Mile Ranch.[8] This was located in the same small valley as the town of Englewood, but on the opposite side of the valley, along with the Englewood School. The hills on this side of the valley were also host to a multitude of mining explorations, the results of which can still be observed today.

Sarah Ann caught wind of the whole affair on Monday the 4th, and left for the Bulldog posthaste. When she arrived at the ranch, she found that her husband had already sold it. Asked where all of her belongings were, the new owner pleaded ignorance. That is when the fair lady pulled out her pistol and shot the man's little finger off. It seems at this point that the new owner suddenly remembered that Joe was going to stash some of the goods at Ten Mile Ranch. So Sarah Ann returned down the road to Deadwood.

Unfortunately, along the way she ran into Paul Rewman, officer of the law, whom she "held up," thinking that he was one of the boys her husband had hired to haul away their belongings. After reaching Ten Mile Ranch she used her pistol to convince the proprietor to drive her stock back out onto the road. She then drove the animals into Deadwood. The story becomes a little lost in the shuffle at this point, and we next find Sarah Ann on Monday the 5th, being arraigned before Justice Clark for stealing a pistol from Bogy's Corral and selling it.

After all the things she had done in the previous days, the only thing they could charge her with was the stolen pistol! She stated that she was under the impression that the gun belonged to her husband and that she

All that remains of the original Bulldog Ranch are several log outbuildings.
PHOTOGRAPHS BY JERRY BRYANT.

had a right to it. Sarah Ann was disarmed before they brought her before the justice, "but whenever she threw her hand behind her the crowd [would] break for the door." She was released on $500 bond while she waited for a decision on the case from the grand jury. Johnny Mahan and Billy Mather paid the bond and the whole town seemed to agree that "the Madam is a whale in fighting her battles. She is bound to have a fair shake, or shoot everybody opposing her."[9]

The brief interlude between arraignment and court date produced only one short article about Sarah Ann, describing her as "one of the most conspicuous personages on the street" and adding that the most common expression used to describe her was that "she's a holy terror." When it came time for Sarah Ann to appear in court on the 13th of August, she was nowhere to be found. Several bail bondsmen, Col. Dunklee and Mr. Carter, were indeed worried, as were the boys who put up her bail. Sarah Ann's attorney, Mr. Watson, reassured everyone that Sarah Ann would arrive, "but at dark that evening she was still *non est*."[10]

While Sarah Ann may not have been available for her court appearance on the 13th, she was able to meet with her husband in Justice Coleman's chambers the next day. It was decided that their joint property would be split evenly and a separation was agreed to. As part of that settlement, the case concerning the theft of the pistol from Bogy's Corral was dropped. The newspapers never did say whatever happened to the bail money from that event.[11]

In most places and most cases that would be the end of it, nothing more would be heard for a while, but such was not the case with our dear Sarah Ann. Two days later she was arrested for attempting to take the life of one John Duckworth. She was held on $500 bond and the case set to be heard by the grand jury. The *Daily Times* now asked its reading public whether it appeared that Sarah Ann was being persecuted. By the time the case actually got to court on September 18, 1879, an additional count of assault with a deadly weapon had been added to her charges. Both charges were dismissed, so perhaps the *Times* was correct, and someone really was out to get Sarah Ann.[12]

Then there was silence. For almost a year nothing was heard of Sarah Ann or her ex. She had bought a new ranch near Pleasant Valley, east of Sturgis.

Tim Coleman had purchased the old Bulldog Ranch, and Sarah Ann's new place was now known as the New Bulldog Ranch. But in September 1880 came a surge of activity, when Joe Erb brought charges against Sarah Ann for bigamy. A new player now enters the scene, Galen Hill.

Galen, also known as Gale, was a local hero of no small fame, when he stopped a bullet during a stage robbery. According to news reports, he was shot through the lungs during the Canyon Springs stage robbery in the fall of 1878, and was nursed back to health under the care of Dr. Babcock. Described as a plucky young man, he won a job as a night watchman as soon as his recovery permitted. In the early part of 1880 we find Galen as an officer of the court, and in September he was given a mission to serve a warrant on Sarah Ann, who had remarried and was now known as Mrs. Hammond. The 1880 census shows a thirty-one-year-old Mrs. Sarah Ann Erb living in the Box Elder Creek area of Lawrence County. She was employing four men at that time, one of whom was twenty-year-old George Hammond, destined to be Sarah Ann's new husband. Young Hammond had made a name for himself in the Black Hills early on when he was arrested for trying to pass off metal filings as gold dust.[13]

When Galen arrived at the New Bulldog Ranch, he rounded up Sarah Ann and George and read the warrant to them, at which time Sarah Ann informed Galen that he had done his duty and would he please get off their property? Galen informed the couple that he did not work that way and that he was determined to escort them both back to Deadwood. This is when George made a run at Galen and attempted to subdue him. Galen came out on top, and the three of them returned to Deadwood.[14]

Over the next few days, as testimony in the preliminary hearing proceeded, an air of scandal hung over the mining camp. The *Black Hills Daily Times* described it thus: "All ready scandal mongers and hoodlums are smacking their lips and rolling their tongues as if gloating on the luscious and daintiest morsels."[15]

It was also at this time that the *Times* recognized a major flaw in the case—specifically, if Sarah Ann was divorced, how could she be a bigamist? It appeared that the worst thing she could be charged with was simple contempt, so the hearing on the case was postponed for two weeks.[16]

When the appointed time for the trial neared, Officer Galen Hill was again dispatched to bring the pair back to Deadwood to face justice. This time things would turn out just a wee bit different, as Sarah Ann met Galen with a long-barreled revolver, and husband George "The Kid" Hammond covered him from behind with a Winchester. Galen surveyed the situation, and prudently decided to withdraw, "not wishing to force any lady, much less the Madame, to accompany him against her will." When Galen arrived back in town, the *Times* ran a brief article surveying the event, which concluded: "Anyone who wishes the distinction and credit of arresting and returning to town [the] ex-Mrs. Erb, can be accommodated by applying to Gale Hill in care of the justices of this city. The Madame still holds the fort."[17]

With so much media attention being given to Sarah Ann, it is not surprising that a certain group of local folks became a little nervous: her creditors, in particular the Fort Meade post trader, W. S. Fanshawe. He heard that Sarah Ann had sold out and was getting ready to skip the country, owing him $700. So Fanshawe sued Sarah Ann in court. Having so recently failed to bring her back to town, the court deputized two new soldiers of the law to go and seek justice at the Bulldog Ranch.

Noah Siever and Tom Faught "took to the warpath" and headed down the Pierre Road to bring the madame to justice. When the boys arrived at the ranch, she treated them in a very lady-like manner. She informed them "that she was very law-abiding and every officer who came to her house and acted like a gentleman would be treated as such, but no man could run a bluff on her, as she was ready to give them as good as they sent."

The boys explained why they were present, and Sarah Ann paid them the money owed to Fanshawe. As they left the ranch that day, there was a strong feeling that the madame was more sinned against than sinning. At the end of September, she showed up in Deadwood and granted the *Times* an audience. She informed them that she had been having all manner of problems since Fanshawe had sued her for her bill at the fort trading post; people had threatened her and attempted to blackmail her. The *Times* relayed her statement to the public at large, that "she has no thought of leaving the country, only to move a short distance. She is prepared to stay and see it out, pay her debts and be well off when her persecutors are fleeing the country."[18] It was noted, and became part of the published record, that the political powers of Lawrence County considered for the last few years the Erb Family as one of its greatest expenses, costing the public an average of $1,000 a year.[19]

In the fall of 1880, a retired Army veterinarian and his friend happened by the Bulldog Ranch No. 2, and met the madame. Nelson Armstrong was taking a prize trotting horse to the Deadwood race track to try to sell her. He was accompanied by a friend who had a few horses to sell, along with a wagonload of butter. Madame Bulldog was in her yard as they passed, and greeted them, explaining that she was the sole proprietress and that she maintained her brace of white bulldogs to protect her chickens from passing freighters, thieves, and vandals. The meeting was brief and uneventful, but provided a glimpse of his mental image of her; stating that she appeared to tip the scales at slightly more than an eighth of a ton.

The entire Fanshawe affair ran rapidly through the court system in November and December, but there was no indication that Sarah Ann was back in town, an event that always drew media attention.[20] The one thing all the court activity did prove was that either Sarah Ann was the most unapproachable of desperados or the legal system was truly being used to persecute her. She was allowed a short vacation from her legal woes, while Thanksgiving and Christmas passed without significant media notice. Then, in January 1881, the trial that everyone was waiting for began: the Territory versus Sarah Ann Erb on one count of bigamy. Joseph Miller defended Sarah Ann, and when all was said and done, twelve men good and true agreed to disagree with that charge.[21] The remainder of 1881 was quiet for Sarah Ann. The *Times* had little to say about her until January 1882, when she appeared in court for buying stolen government buffalo coats.[22]

In February 1882, the paper advised that Sarah Ann had harvested and stored a large amount of ice at the Bulldog ranch near Sturgis.[23] Also in 1882, Sarah Ann opened a saloon in Deadwood named, of course, The Bulldog. The *Times* noted that the sign for the saloon was unique and just as appropriate, with a "painting of a bulldog with the usual heavy jaws and a stump of a tail."[24]

The opening of her saloon probably coincided with the sale of Bulldog Ranch No. 2, to Dow Waln, one of the earliest pioneers in the Black Hills.[25]

March brought Sarah Ann back to court again. This time it was for having "purchased and appropriated for her own use, goods and stores belonging to the United States, knowing at the time of purchase that they so belonged." She was found not guilty, which did not sit well with the editor of the *Times*, or so it would seem. "We would not attempt to say as to whether or not the prosecution has proved their case," the *Times* opined, "nor are we inclined to strike below the belt, in this particular instance, yet we will say that if the defendant isn't a bad woman, on general principles, then personal appearance will justify a suit against nature for libel."[26]

Two days later she was back yet again, on a similar charge, and this time a soldier named Conroy was also implicated.[27] She was held over to stand trial. Then on March 20 she was in front of a judge again, this time for assault and battery. The case was ordered to the grand jury.[28] The final word on Sarah Ann came in late August, when the *Times* noted that she was seen dealing stud poker in Miles City, Montana Territory.[29]

Sarah Ann's woes during the year of 1882 seem to have marked the end of her period of infamy, and nothing else was heard from her, at least not in the Deadwood news, from then on.

Sarah Ann's ex-husband Joe Erb also vanished without a trace, but not George Hammond. George went from passing brass filings to protecting the honor of our notorious madame, and then on to, of all things, teaching school. His name stands out in the records as a member of the Fifth Annual Lawrence County Teacher's Institute in December 1889.[30] Well, he was quite young when Sarah Ann first captured him—he must have learned a lot.

CHAPTER SEVEN

MOLLIE JOHNSON: QUEEN OF THE BLONDES

All the young women "students" or "boarders" who lodged at Madam Mollie's place peroxided their hair bright blonde, in keeping with Mollie's trademark. While the newspapers ran breathless stories of the group's scandalous doings, newsmen also regularly praised the madam's community spirit.

Late in the evening on a hot night in August 1879, an anonymous newspaper reporter walked up Sherman Street. When he arrived at the corner of Sherman and Lee, the establishment run by Madam Mollie Johnson, he found pleasant cause for pause. He wrote:

> *At the dead of night when all nature is hushed asleep, this reporter is frequently regaled, while on his way home, by the gentle cadence of sweet songs which floats out upon the stillness of the gulch like the silvery horns of Elf land faintly blowing. Vocal music, wherever heard or by whatever produced is entrancing to this sinner. Hence the aforesaid sounds are sure to arrest his step at the corner and compel him to lend his ear to the mellifluent melody, which steals out from Molly Johnson's Harem. But he does not draw*

any nearer, for he knows that where the sirens dwell you linger in ——, that their songs are death, but——destruction please; and he travels on, disgusted with himself because his virtuous life possesses such a skeleton of fun, yet wonders that such a voluptuous harmony is tolerated by the divine muse of song to leave such a bad place.[1]

The article seems to echo the prevalent public sentiment but simultaneously seems to pose the question of why. Why if something is so bad is it allowed to prevail, flourish, and indeed flaunt its very veil of sin for everyone to see? It was true, Mollie Johnson, known as the "Queen of the Blondes," had a knack for flaunting it. Renting a $10-an-hour carriage, she would drag the main streets of Deadwood, snubbing and sneering at all the soiled doves who did not work for her.[2]

From the beginning it seems as though Deadwood had a love/hate relationship with Mollie; on one hand she would be publicly scorned, and on the other hand they would write: "The largest crowd of bald headed men we ever saw assembled in Deadwood, gathered in front of the Sidney Stage Office [service from Sidney, Nebraska] last night upon arrival of the coach. They expected to see Madame Mollie Johnson alight with bevy of bankers' daughters, but the coach came in flying light, and a more disappointed mob would be difficult to imagine. The reception committee had took the girls from the coach near Crook and brought them to the city by private conveyance."

"Concerned" would actually be a mild word to describe how Deadwood felt about the welfare of Mollie's business affairs. When two of Mollie's girls ran away, of course it made the news. Were citizens cheering for the girls, or wondering what would Mollie do?

Then there was the great buggy race that occurred on the prairie flats between Crook City and Deadwood. Mollie and her girls had attended a baseball game at Fort Meade that day, consuming perhaps a little more "Rosy" than they should have. The girls rented two light buggies from Patton in Deadwood for the trip and decided that a little race was in order. Some combination of the high velocity of the buggies, a general lack of experience with the reins, the rolling nature of the prairie, and the alcohol content of the Rosy caused the buggies to collide. There in a heap of petticoats and splinters, Mollie discovered that one of their racing crew was seriously injured. After she flagged down a passing citizen (and one can't imagine there were many), one buggy was made fit for the trail, and in a total stranger's company, the injured Miss Flora Belle was conveyed to Deadwood for medical attention, "leaving the Madam and the other golden haired sirens afoot upon the boundless prairie. In the meantime night dropped her sable curtain down and pinned it with a star, and our three heroines like Hagar were left crying in the wilderness."

It does not take long for news of this sort to travel in a female-deprived male environment, and soon "three well-known young men of Deadwood, mounted on broncos, hove into sight and taking in the plight of the trio invited them to a seat behind their saddles." The girls arrived back in town long after the "last heathen had bit his pipe a closing lick," and noted that Mollie, in her position behind the saddle, "did not resemble a fairy riding on a floating thistle-down. In fact she resembled anything else in the world but that."

In addition to publishing amusing tales of the everyday lives of Mollie and her girls, the *Times* also spent a certain amount of time baiting the girls in hopes of creating a newsworthy cat fight. In one such incident, the paper attempted to pit three of Mollie's competitors against her. It all started with the arrest of Sis Clinton, Iva Redmond, and Edith St. Clair by Assistant Deputy U.S. Marshal Spencer for selling hooch without a license. In a brief, page 4 accusation, the *Times* indicated that Mollie had provided the information that had "caused the corralling of her lascivious sisters, and it was the opinion of the average rounder that Madam Mollie is fixing up a good pounding for herself—by the trio of female sinners referred to."

The next day Mollie sent the *Times* a short note stating, "I know nothing of the ladies referred to. I am the last one to do injury to these ladies, or as you say, my sisters in sin." The *Times* countered this by stating that they were "glad that Mollie's skirts are clean of suspicion," but that their information was obtained from "Hugh J. Campbell, United States District Attorney for Dakota Territory." But that was the last they wrote about the incident. The real question that begs to be answered here is, why was the *Times* so keen on directing retribution and justice among a small group of marginalized people that they considered so very bad?

In the beginning, Mollie was not afraid of Deadwood's legal system and, on several occasions, had unruly customers arrested. She always tried to follow up by pressing charges and sending the erring males to court. An example of what it would have cost a man to rough up one of Mollie's girls was evident when William Ward appeared in front of Judge Coleman for assault and battery on one of them. Ward was fined $5 and costs. It was noted by the *Times* that he was seen that evening "rustling to raise that amount in order to keep out of the cooler."

When the *Times* was unable to find enough fodder to enflame a ruckus between the girls, they tried to work up the other newspapers with accusations about the girls. A summary of one article goes something like this: When the train left Omaha Station on February 8, 1880, a young man and a young lady, seated at opposite ends of the car, met for the first time and proceeded to scandalize the rest of the passengers. Prior to meeting the young man, the lady in question had told a fellow passenger that she was on her way to Deadwood to marry an old beau, who had come west several years before and had struck it rich. For much of the day, the young lady and the gent played cards, laughed, and whispered to each other.

Other passengers made it their business to watch over the assumed betrothed young girl and were amazed when at one point the young man abruptly got up and went to his seat at the other end of the car. At which time the girl requested that the porter make up her bunk. A short time later the train pulled into the station and the young man got off, and was not seen getting back on the train. Meanwhile the young lady went off to her bed.

Several of the passengers had spoken to the young man before he had met the girl, and he had informed them that he had property in Nevada and was in fact on his way there. So the passengers began to talk; a decision was made that the young man must have sneaked back onto the train and was presently only a few yards away, in the bunk of the betrothed young lady. The conductor was notified, the porter was notified, and together they proceeded to her bunk and threw open the curtain, only to have the young man tumble out in his red flannel underwear. The *Pioneer* made comments concerning how brash the young man was, but the real condemnation came to the girl, whose exact arrival time on the Sidney stage was noted. It included an additional note stating what they would do if "they" were the girl's intended.

The very next day, the *Times* produced an article condemning the *Pioneer* for having dedicated a third of its Sunday social page to the exploits of one of Mollie Johnson's girls, calling it "demoralizing Sunday reading for the family." They then went on to say that the reason was obvious why the *Times* had not "raised its editorial hands in horror."

Perhaps no small part of the positive side of the papers' and the girls' relationship was generosity. The *Times* had a habit of publishing articles concerning the plights that some of the gulch's citizenry would find themselves in, often through no fault of their own. Right above this article would be a list of locals who had contributed, titled "By the fruits of their etc." or "Bread Cast upon the Waters." Mollie's name was always on the list. The same could be said for other charities, as she was a known supporter of Irish Famine Relief. But what does that say of Mollie's "American-ness"?

A glimpse at the 1880 territorial census tells something of her past. Mollie was born in Alabama. She had declared herself a widow and had told the enumerator that she was twenty-seven years old. The document also showed that she was living with five young ladies, ages nineteen to twenty-seven and from all over North America: Massachusetts, New York, Missouri, Michigan, and Canada.

The *Times* and other organs of local news often followed the Madam's activities with what seemed like stern concern as she hosted dances and "balls" in the firehouse, in this warehouse or that. And while everyone seemed to agree that she was an absolutely bad person, everyone watched the show, and always stated that her get-togethers were ideally suited for the stranger in town.

When I first encountered Mollie in Deadwood's newspapers of February 1878, she was getting married to Lew Spencer, a singing comedian at the Bella Union Theatre in Deadwood. The Reverend Mr. Norcross performed the service, much to the amazement of Lew's friends, who somehow just could not picture him as a married man. There seems to be no sure way to tell how the marriage went or even to what duration it could claim, but whoever was married to Lew in 1879 got shot in Denver by Lew, and he went to prison for the offense. The local newspapers provided ample evidence that Mollie was very much alive well into the 1880s and in the Deadwood area, still throwing ruckus parties for her admiring and paying friends. As for that wife-shooter Lew, Colorado did not hang him. After he was released from prison, he went on to record the earliest known version of "A Hot Time in the Old Town" in 1896. The song became so popular that Roosevelt's Rough Riders used it as a theme song.

It was a sad day in September 1879 when the greater part of Deadwood burnt to the ground. Folks who were able to save some of their things packed them in trunks and carried them uphill to safety, only to have thieves steal them. Mollie's house—both her home and place of business—was on the corner of Sherman and Lee streets, one of the areas that received ample warning. She might have saved the chairs, the china, or perhaps even the silver and glass. But no, she would not move a thing until she was sure that Jennie Phillips was safe, although Jennie was entirely beyond saving. Jennie had died the day before, and was resting in her coffin in Mollie's parlor. As the roof of the Madam's house burst into flame Jennie was loaded into a hearse and taken a safe distance up City Creek, where she remained until she could be buried the next day on Mount Moriah. Mollie's place was a total loss. While some merchants moaned over the loss of $3,000 or $4,000 in the fire, Mollie contributed $7,000 to the flames that day.

Just exactly who was Miss Jennie Phillips to receive such attention from the madam? Well, for one thing, she was not a Jennie at all, she was actually a Josephine. Josephine Willard, to be exact, and she had been the only child of a Chicago family. Her father ran a successful business selling saddlery hardware. By all accounts, she had cast off a life of much luxury only to end up as one of the madam's girls. The description that the newspaper ran of the atmosphere in the Johnson house on the day before the great fire is a snapshot of Victorian mourning. "Upon calling at the house yesterday morning," the paper reported, "we found the pictures on the wall, all turned inward, the girls with grief stricken faces standing around like frightened children, and the Madam, who referred to the dead as 'my little girl' bowed in sorrow that was evidently genuine.

Jennie had been sick for only a short time before dying, and the only clue of its cause is a short article written a few months before her death, meant to entertain the good citizens of the community. It appears the keeper of the toll road just below Fountain City kept a cat. Said cat was chained to a tree near the toll road. On a warm July day, out for a Sunday ride, Jennie and several of her lady friends were coming down the toll road on their way to Crook City. As they passed through the tollgate, Jennie "espied the critter." Reaching down, she picked the cat up and attempted to give it a kiss. The cat, not really used to such attention, panicked, and bit our poor Jennie through both lips. Could this have been the kiss of death for Jennie?

Mollie's girls did not seem to learn much from the great Deadwood Fire, for exactly a year later the *Times* ran an article about a fire at Mollie's place that started in one of her upstairs chambers. It appears that one of girls was a little chilly, and thought that by stacking her firewood behind the stove it would be dryer and so would burn better and hotter. So there it was, a stack of nice dry firewood behind a stove. Poof, it caught on fire and then the wall was on fire. First on the scene was the South Deadwood Hose Team, and it was a cold night when no one else was about. The Deadwood team was still hooking up to the hydrant as the Homestake crew arrived. Meanwhile, the investigating party had rushed into the house, discovered the cause and doused the fire with a few well-placed buckets of water. As we do today, the Deadwood folks back then recognized their fire fighters as heroes who came to the front regardless of the time or the weather. The *Times* went on to note that this was the second such fire to start at Mollie's house recently, the first being a chimney fire.

It's not always clear just where morality stood in early Deadwood. All the newspapers would hoot and carry on about the sinful activities of this person or that lady of soiled repute. One fine day, Mollie decided that her girls needed a finer place to live in and conduct business, so she sold the old house to a hard-working woman who wanted to use it as a boarding house. Down came Mollie's traditional lantern and up went the new one that advertised "lodging." Not a single day passed before the *Times* ran the following news brief, "A sinful place, a resort for naughty men, on lower Sherman Street, has a lantern in front of it bearing this unique device, 'Lodging'."

The very next day another article ran, bubbling with apologies to the "Lodging's" new owner, Mrs. K. J. White, "an estimable lady, who, we are

Shocking to today's sensibilities, many prostitutes began their careers as teens. Madams advertised their wares with photographic cards such as these.

H·R· LOCKE & Co.
Deadwood, So. Dakota.

glad to state is keeping neat and respectable lodging rooms there." The *Times* went on to say that they had thought Madam Mollie had put up the new lantern as ploy to catch "Tenderfeet."

With episodes such as this inspiring the *Daily News*, who would have ever dreamed that the *Times* would have advocated that two of the city's young daughters be turned over to Madam Johnson by their mothers and the law? But it happened. The unfortunate young ladies, a Miss Pettijohn and a Miss Woodall, were the hellraisers of the day on Deadwood's streets. The article went on to tell how the mothers of these girls had done everything, including chaining them up, to mend their evil ways—all to no avail. Thus, a promiscuous ball was arranged in Central City, which the girls attended. At the time prescribed by the girls' mothers, they were arrested without ceremony and conducted to Mollie's place, where she accepted them as boarders. The *Times*, to justify such recruitment, stated that:

> *In justice to Madam Mollie, we must say that she would never be a party to the ruin of a young girl. On the contrary, it is recorded to her credit she has assisted foolish girls by money and advice to lead a pure and virtuous life, but these young dames were all beyond aid. They were bad eggs, so bad that nothing could spoil them, and she accepted them as boarders. We are not so certain but this change is a benefit all around. They are now publicly known for what they are. Therefore, they cannot contaminate other girls. At Madam Mollie's house they will have to preserve external decency in speech and action. We cannot congratulate Miss Pettijohn or Miss Woodall on their new departure, but we hope now that they are in a house [where] they will forget the brutal indecency they learned and practiced on the streets.*

As time passed, Mollie began to travel more often, and the *Times* either lost interest in her or moved on to memorialize some other poor soul's life. One of the last articles that the *Times* wrote about her concerned her travels. Mollie was Deadwood-bound on the Sidney stage in March 1881, and because of the time of year and the nature of road construction at that period of area development, the roads were rough and treacherous. The roads were so bad that at almost every stage stop some of Mollie's trunks had to be left behind. One of her trunks was left at the Little Cottonwood Station.

Mike Haley, who had a band of horses at Big Cottonwood, went on a drinking spree and went to Little Cottonwood, where he proceeded to break into one of Mollie's trunks. For reasons that forever will only be known only to Mike, he gathered up a large amount of Mollie's clothing and took it back to his place. The stage messengers thought that he might have been the culprit, so they went to his place and found the goods. "He felt so badly over what he had done that he said he would not survive the disgrace. He took poison—strychnine—and as the coach passed there on Tuesday last he was in spasms, and has probably gone over the range."

As with any such business, Mollie's all-girl boarding house had its ups and downs, petty jealousies, and infighting, which apparently brought an end to Mollie's reign as Deadwood's Queen of the Blondes. A brief article by the *Daily Times* started like this: "Judge Giddings, the fat man who holds the scales of the blind goddess in Deadwood proper, had but little to claim his attention yesterday." The article continued to say that one Mollie's female students, Anna Bennett, had filed a complaint against her and two others for the larceny of a number of silk dresses and other items. The judge signed the warrant and sent out the court's fearless but shy defender, Galen Hill who, despite being "bashful, he did his duty by arresting the whole caboodle." The *Daily Times* hoped that it would suffer no inconvenience over Mollie's arrest.

From that point on, Mollie's name became little more than a note in the background as she arrived and departed Deadwood by stage for the occasional struggle with litigation. Her final mention noted her departure from Deadwood on January 29, 1883.

CHAPTER EIGHT

ELIZABETH LOVELL: AMAZON OF ELIZABETHTOWN

"Wilder than a wild owl," Elizabeth trusted no man, and she made that quite clear—gun in hand—time and again. Especially when one of the lying creatures came onto any of her mining claims. Despite all that, one faithful (if silent) male remained devoted to her.

Elizabeth Lovell was a fascinating woman who, had she lived a little longer, would have rivaled Calamity Jane in pure frontier spunk and firepower. Today we wonder whether she was a deeply disturbed soul who lost her life in a cry for help, or just an intolerant woman who would not bear any man to do her wrong. What follows combines the contemporary observations of two independent Deadwood newspapers on the scene.

The first mention of Elizabeth came in 1877, when she appeared in front of Justice Baker on a charge of malicious mischief. She had demolished her neighbor's fence. Justice Baker gave Elizabeth a sound lecture and sent her home after telling her to never do anything like that again.[1]

The following January, Elizabeth was back in the news. She published notice of a new claim location, the Lloyd lode,[2] while another article launched her reputation as a shootist, describing a confrontation that began when a group of miners laid claim to a piece of land that Elizabeth believed she had legal rights to. By January 15, when Elizabeth arrived on the scene, the miners had opened an adit and installed a windlass at its portal. The claim was known as the Mother Lode so naturally the paper put two and two together and came up with "Mother" Lovell protecting the Mother Lode. It went a little further than an argument over ownership when Elizabeth pulled her "six-shooter with the four inch barrel." As may be expected, her opponents retreated in great disarray, then Elizabeth "knocked the windlass back into the open shaft." In the process of this activity, Elizabeth's "Howitzer exploded tearing a hole in Mrs. Lovell's dress."[3]

Elizabeth was summoned before the grand jury at the end of April, charged with malicious mischief, but the jury took no action.[4]

By early May, she had been in front of the judge four times for four different legal infractions. On the 7th she made the front page again when she stormed a mining camp. "The Amazon of Elizabethtown was out on the shoot again this morning with her little gun, storming the position of a couple of miners, who she claimed, were working her ground. When the miners, who knew of her belligerent nature, saw her marching on their works, they deserted and fell back in great disorder." The article went on to say that Elizabeth had already been arrested, and had at least three prior times been arrested for attacking weak parties of men who attempted to fool around her property.[5]

Elizabethtown, by the way, was not named for Elizabeth Lovell but instead was named for its first female resident, Elizabeth Card.

Only two months later, Elizabeth was on the front page again. On Monday, June 24, she had threatened to shoot another of Elizabethtown's male citizens, soon after which she barricaded herself in her home. The entire mess was the result of a long-standing dispute over ownership of a small cabin in Elizabethtown. John Tomby claimed to be the cabin's legal owner, and so did Elizabeth. That evening, Elizabeth noted that Tomby was not at the cabin. She proceeded to arm herself and take possession of the building, where she awaited Tomby's return. When Tomby came home later that night, he was met at the door by Elizabeth and her "Little Gun." He promptly abandoned the claim and went to fill out a warrant for her arrest. A description of Elizabeth's general activities were also given in this article as: "She gets out on the War Path about so often, and she goes for some big bulldozing brute of a man with her little gun, and when she turns loose she makes them skip too, for there is blood on the moon." The headline read, "ELIZABETH TO THE FRONT—CASTLE LOVELL BARRICADED."[6]

Early the next morning, officers Storm and Brewer, followed by a vast assemblage of other law enforcement folks, approached the Lovell residence with the intent of serving a warrant for Elizabeth's arrest. When Officer Storm demanded entrance, Elizabeth refused. He then asked that she come to the window so he could read the warrant to her. Again she refused—not an inch would she move from her fortified position in the hallway of her home. Officers of the law and some friendly neighbors tried to persuade her to come out, but to no avail.

She proclaimed that she would never be taken alive. The folks trying to take her in made numerous promises concerning her safety, but their words fell on deaf ears. Elizabeth stated that men had made promises to her before, and she would not be fooled into believing that any man knows how to tell the truth, especially in the Hills. The officers negotiated for several more hours and then returned to the city for rest and a drink. On their return the next morning, they were accompanied by several hundred onlookers who were amused that the law seemed powerless against this single woman.[7] On the third day of the siege, a $100 reward was offered for her capture.[8]

The following day, a court-appointed lawyer, Addison W. Hastie, arrived at her front door convinced that he could persuade her to put down her arms and accompany him to the county jail.[9] With smiles and soft words he encouraged her to open the door, and at last she did. Elizabeth, armed with two cocked pistols in one hand and a large Navy revolver in the other, informed him that she was ready for business. "This formidable and unexpected war like array of death dealing implements knocked the General's smiles into expressions of fear, and instead of presenting the most smiling front that was ever seen in the hills, he showed up the scaredest looking mug conceivable and retreated at the first opportunity." Hastie's final statement on the subject was that "she looked wilder than a wild owl, and that no amount of smiles will ever capture her—she is too

Elizabethtown as it appeared in 1890. COURTESY DEADWOOD HISTORY, INC., DEADWOOD, SD.

old to be taken in by that sort of foolishness, and a different strategy must be employed to corral her."[10]

At this point, the authorities noted certain peculiarities with the charge that had been leveled against Ms. Lovell, and all charges were dropped. Does this mean that Elizabeth had a just claim and was vindicated? John Tomby seemed to have had enough of the whole affair, and put the piece of land and its cabin up for sale. It was not on the market very long when a fellow by the name of Francis Johnson bought it near the end of July. All the newspaper accounts of this incident seem to agree that Johnson knew exactly what he was buying into—big trouble in a dress.

Soon after the purchase, Elizabeth found Johnson busy tearing down the fence that she herself had constructed to protect what she viewed as her cabin. She marched out to the fence and began telling Johnson that he was making a great mistake. Johnson told her where she could go, and both parties went for their guns but Elizabeth was a little faster and got the drop on Johnson. He was still in the process of pulling his revolver from his belt when Elizabeth aimed at his vitals and shot him from a distance of four feet. The ball struck the lower part of the knuckle of his little finger and exited at the back of his wrist. It then perforated his shirt, made a circuit of his right side then went across the street where it narrowly missed the head of an onlooker.

At this point, Elizabeth—thinking that her business was finished—retired to her house.[11] Johnson finished drawing his revolver and got off two shots at the retreating woman, one narrowly missing her head before she disappeared through the door. On June 30, a brief article noted that the charges against Elizabeth had been dropped because Judge Charles E. Barker had determined the shooting to be in self-defense.[12]

On October 11, 1878, one paper ran a short article that jokingly suggested that Elizabeth should run for sheriff because of her past record. The same article also nominated "Negro General" Samuel Fields, as Register of Deeds, because he was always on hand, and Frenchy the Bottle Fiend for treasurer because he was such a good collector.[13]

On that same day, John Rogers went to court on charges of malicious mischief. Rogers owned a claim next to Elizabeth's. It appears that Rogers had been working his claim when the problem arose. He was sinking a shaft, and taking the waste rock and dumping it into a partially collapsed shaft—which was on Elizabeth's claim. Elizabeth arrived on the scene and ordered Rogers to cease and desist. "He having the fear of man, and in this case worse than man—woman—before his eyes, did as commanded." Elizabeth was not satisfied with Rogers' merely stopping; she wanted him to pay for the damages she would incur having her mineshaft emptied. So she filed charges against him. The results of the court case were not published, but based on the happenings over the next few days it would be safe to say that Elizabeth was not happy with the results.[14]

On October 14, Johnny Rogers and his friend, a night watchman named Bennett, sat on the front porch of Johnny's home, which adjoined Elizabeth Lovell's digs. The shortest route for Johnny to get to his house was across Elizabeth's land, and she had warned him on several occasions that she felt it would be much better for his health if he found a different route. Bennett was the first of the pair to see Elizabeth coming, and he told Johnny that she looked upset and that he was in all likelihood going to have to shoot her. Johnny then said, "I can't shoot a woman," as he left the porch, going inside the house to avoid her. Hot on his trail, Elizabeth followed Johnny inside his own home. She caught up with him and placed the pistol to his breast and fired, point blank. After shooting Johnny, Elizabeth tuned and fled back down the hill. Johnny, not realizing how serious his wound was, grabbed Bennett's revolver, made for the front door and fired four shots at the retreating Elizabeth. The last of Johnny's shots is the only one that hit Elizabeth, but it entered the back of her head and exited through her left eye.[15]

Amazingly, Elizabeth lived for forty-five minutes after being shot. Johnny Rogers lingered near death for several days, under the care of Dr. Dickinson. The bullet had entered his body near the apex of his heart and was still lodged in his body cavity. That evening, Dr. Dickinson stated that Johnny's wound appeared to be mortal though there was a slim chance that he might survive.

Like most good subjects for a local legend, Elizabeth was not yet in the ground when tales of her deeds and misdeeds began to be spun. The *Times* immediately began casting about for someone to blame, naming Officer Beaman, who had held her in custody for threatening the life of

One entrepeneur established a toll house on the road entering Elizabethtown. Today, the same location is occupied by the SpringHill Suites hotel. COURTESY DEADWOOD HISTORY, INC., DEADWOOD, SD.

John Rogers, then released her on $300 bond. In the courtroom after the judge had ordered Rogers' release, Elizabeth swore to shoot John Rogers and hang three or four other men. Still she was released. The *Times* stated that ninety-nine percent of local residents, and all of the officers of the law, had been convinced that she should have been cared for rather than shot.[16] It listed those citizens who had been declared insane by the courts since January 1878, beginning with "Uncle" Billy Coffin. In June of that year, the probate court had ordered three people committed to an insane asylum, and they were transported there by Noah Siever.[17] But Elizabeth Lovell never received such consideration.

Before Elizabeth was buried, Street Commissioner (cleaner) Patrick Early petitioned the probate court to be made Special Administrator of Elizabeth's estate. He immediately proceeded to take possession of the estate. When the books were examined by a representative of the press in April 1879, it was discovered that Elizabeth's assets were just sufficient to cover the burial costs and final medical expenses. Mr. Early was discharged, his duties completed. Further investigations indicated that Elizabeth's assets had actually been more in the neighborhood of $2,000, an amount much in excess of what it took to bury her. It also became apparent that her burial had not been paid for, nor had her burial clothes, nor the coffin. Also unaccounted for were her fine gold pocket watch and chain, a diamond necklace, and a valuable pin. Included in the estate had been several city lots in Elizabethtown, her home, furniture, and her mining claims. All appeared lost to the shenanigans of Mr. Early.[18]

But a legend is really never lost. Articles ran in the *Times* and the *Pioneer* until a final story was published in December 1881 when a fellow named Butler was reassigned as the administrator of Elizabeth's estate.[19] And who, we may ask, was Butler? Well, Mr. S. T. Butler is the fellow who realized that there was a fox in the hen house when it came to the handling of Elizabeth's estate.[20] Butler did all the investigations that ended by placing Mr. Early in front of a judge to explain his gross mishandling of Elizabeth's assets. What of the gold watch and chain? It seems that Mr. Early had given them to Mrs. Early, and during Mr. Butler's investigation they were relinquished to the court.[21] And the diamonds? They eventually ended up on display—at Butler's Jewelry Store.[22]

. . . And Benjamin Murch, the Man Who Loved Her

Elizabeth Lovell had arrived in Deadwood in the company of a man named Benjamin Murch back in May 1877. She first opened a restaurant and then went into mining, with Murch as her silent partner. A few folks noticed Murch here and there doing Elizabeth's bidding, but when it came to violence he stepped aside.

At the peak of Elizabeth's bout with Johnny Rogers, the *Black Hills Daily Times* demanded to know the whereabouts of that "old man" who was always hanging around Lovell. In no way was he ever implicated in Elizabeth's tirades, though he was never far from her side. And he was there when she died.

A somewhat quiet man, oftentimes unseen, Murch had co-patented the Lloyd mining claim with Elizabeth. After the great fire of 1879, he was required to prove that he was actually half owner of the claim because all of the records in the courthouse had burned. Ultimately, he had to purchase Elizabeth's share of the claim from her estate. Things seemed to spiral downhill from there—items he had assumed were his were reclaimed by the estate and the courts demanded their return, among them some of Elizabeth's diamonds. By the end of 1880, Murch was struggling to hold on to his claim; with no promise of money on the horizon he took a job as the janitor for the county courthouse. When not busy with that duty, he would try to work the claim by himself.

In October 1880, a dispute arose between Benjamin Murch and one of his neighbors, Joe Vollin. To be more precise, the *Times* described Vollin as a neighbor of Elizabeth's old nemesis, Johnny Rogers. The dispute was not over mining rights, but surrounded a spring that Murch claimed was on his mineral claim.

Vollin, on the other hand, thought the spring was on his land, and had given his neighbors free access to improve the spring and use its water. Thus the neighborhood had joined in to dig it out and generally clean up the area. Murch had a prospect uphill, and as he worked the claim, dirt and rocks fell down into the spring, muddying it to the point that it was no longer usable. When the neighbors complained to Vollin, he rushed to the scene. Immediately an argument ensued between the two men, and soon it degenerated into a fistfight. Soon many of the men living in the area joined together and physically removed Murch from the site.

On a cold night in January 1881, a group of masked men burst into Murch's cabin. This is where the story gets difficult. The masked "Vigilantes" claimed that they induced Murch to disrobe and then covered his body with warm tar. Murch's version of the story was that the group of masked hooligans from a Bad Lands–district saloon shoved their way into his cabin. Not liking the décor, they gave his front door a good slathering of hot tar then coated it with feathers. Though the men wore masks, Murch said he recognized many of their voices.

The deed supposedly was done in vigilante retribution because Murch was thought to have lured a young girl from Lead City into his cabin with candy, where it was assumed that he had had his way with her. Up in arms, the *Times* said "If it [justice] can be done in no other way than Vigilantes, we say, let them do it."

Boldly, the Vigilantes posted a letter to the sheriff in the same issue, saying that they had indeed tarred and feathered Murch, and this would not be the end of it. A few days later, in a separate article, the editors warned the "Old Rake," who was trying to cause trouble for the citizens who tarred and feathered him, that it could have been much worse, citing the case of a man and woman in New York, who had each been sentenced to twelve years in prison for abducting an immigrant girl and forcing her into prostitution. All of which smacks of barroom hypocrisy, considering the number of madams and brothels in Deadwood, not to mention that major force of kidnapped virtue, Al Swearingen, wandering the streets of Deadwood unscathed.

Time passed and the dust appeared to settle for almost a year, then Murch was back in the news again. Now it was not young girls, but rather a problem that had been allowed to go on for years. A *Times* article began, "This city is now remarkably free of disturbing elements, but still one individual remains, by the name of Murch, who has a most unsavory reputation." The article rehashed past accusations, then brought up the real gist of the piece, the fresh-water spring near Murch's mineral claim. Murch had been working his claim and again sullied the spring, raising the hackles of all his neighbors. The *Times* proclaimed that Murch should be awarded the medal for Mean Man of the Hills.

Working what most people considered a barren mining claim did not earn Murch a lot of friends or money, so he kept his job as courthouse janitor and repaired roads for the county. Several times locals tried to have his claim declared abandoned so they could acquire it, but in the end all was lost to taxes, and Murch was relegated to the county poor house in Gayville.

Murch languished in these quarters for many years before he died, and only then was his story discovered by the American media. During his last year, he told the story of his arrival in Deadwood with Elizabeth Lovell, a woman who had captured his heart. Murch thought that she was perhaps the most adventurous and determined woman ever to come to the Black Hills. He related with marked accuracy the circumstances of Lovell's death, the results of which turned him into a bum with no cause to continue life, starting his downward spiral to the poor house. After more than a decade in the county poor house, Benjamin Murch died on August 17, 1908. Three days later, his story was reprinted in newspapers across the nation.[23]

JUSTIN CACHLIN: FRENCHY THE BOTTLE FIEND

The old Frenchman didn't bathe or changes clothes too often, lived in abject poverty, and compulsively gathered up the numerous bottles and cigar butts thrown onto Deadwood's streets. Everyone enjoyed laughing at his craziness without realizing what a useful citizen he really was.

The future "bottle fiend" of Deadwood, Justin Cachlin, was born in France in 1817 (give or take a year). By the time that the United States declared war on Mexico thirty years later, he was living in New Orleans. Justin volunteered and became part of the Third New Orleans Cavalry Regiment. Under the command of Captain Deploe, Justin served with distinction for the duration of the war and then was mustered out.

His travels in the army had opened his eyes to the multitude of opportunities on the western frontier. After he became a civilian in 1848, he began traveling throughout the West, particularly in California, Nevada, and Montana. He was rumored to have made at least one fortune in Nevada and Montana.

Justin's brothers were not so fortunate. A Deadwood paper stated that they were poor and were raising large families so Justin split his wealth with his family, investing his share in mining speculation. It may be that he lost all his money.[1]

The first known written verification of Justin's existence was his voter registration in California in 1870 where he declared that he was a naturalized American citizen, born in France, and fifty-three years old. With little or nothing left of his fortune, Justin joined Henry Mundy's expedition of prospectors and entered the Black Hills in 1876.

He initially prospected in the Custer area, but was not very satisfied with what he saw there. He told the Hillyo (Hill City) camp that there probably was not enough gold in the area to make it pay, and even if there had been, there wasn't enough water to work it, and the fall of the creek was insufficient for either hydraulicking or sluicing. The Hillyo boys all felt like Justin should be hanged right on the spot, and had he not been so well respected by two of the camp "wheels," Captain Munson and Captain Dodson, Justin's story would have ended right there. The two men not only vouched for Justin, but Captain Munson also agreed with everything he said.

Heading north from Hillyo, Justin arrived in Deadwood in 1877, and, we see in newspaper accounts of that period that he was not yet known as Frenchy nor was he noted as being a bottle fiend (that is, addicted to bottle-collecting). Early that year Justin had staked a claim and was sinking a shaft in it. By May, he had enough money and prospects that he hired a lawyer and took two men, Alfred Howard and William Lynn, before Justice Gooding for having destroyed a house that he owned over a mine shaft on his property. Then, in the first week of June, he took William Aylmer to court for assault and battery. He won the case and the man was fined and made to pay court costs.[2] That is nearly the last we see of "Justin the miner," in the Deadwood newspapers.[3]

Nearly a year later, Justin was being called "Old Frenchy, the Bottle Fiend." A paper stated that he recently "exhausted his entire vocabulary of English and French swear words on a little boy that had attempted to sell him a collection of bottles. The little fellow dropped his bottles and cut through the storm like a snow bird."[4] From then on, hardly a week would pass without some jocular note or another appearing in the *Times* or the *Pioneer* concerning Frenchy's whereabouts or activities.

The second 1878 newspaper appearance of The Bottle Fiend gives the reader a sketchy but indelible image of Frenchy's daily circuit of Deadwood's dirt streets. "Wes Travis created a stampede to his horse sale by a new dodge," the paper reported. "He attached the Old French Bottle Fiend's sack of calamities to a pony's tail and allowed it [the pony] to kick it loose. The trick was very successful in attracting a crowd."[5]

Besides his ever-present bottle-collecting bag, he sported some intriguing selections in daily attire, which oddly enough changed from time to time. In 1879, the *Times* commented on Justin's latest summer style when he showed up on Main Street with a pair of pants that had a tin pan in the seat for carrying ice. The *Times* editor noted, tongue in cheek, that the pants were the latest in summer style and "Frenchy" had had them imported from Cincinnati.[6]

By then, Justin seemed to have developed a habit of claiming almost anything that was lying about, not just bottles. On several occasions, apparently believing that clothing left dangling on the line to dry overnight were abandoned, he would help himself. There were several complaints, but nothing was mentioned until the following February when Sheriff John Manning spied a pair of pants that looked really, *really* familiar, parading down Main Street on Justin's legs. Another onlooker, Charley Spencer, was so taken with the pants that he tried to buy them, but Justin smugly told him they were not for sale. The local citizenry agreed with the sheriff, though, that the pants were by then beyond rescue, and Justin was allowed to go on his way.[7]

Frenchy's home, as well as his appearance, came into the newspaper spotlight when the editor of the *Times* apologized for ignoring "an eminent citizen and justly celebrated character of the town." A *Times* reporter had hiked up City Creek during a quest to rectify this wrong. The description went this way:

> *the chateau of this antiquarian is located on one of the romantic situations of City Creek, below a bridge at the foot of a declivity,*

descending which, unless the pedestrian rears well back in his "breeching," his pedal continuations will fly from under him. The drainage of a stable ladens the air with sultry odors, while the incense of a thousand gunny sacks, cod fish boxes and aromatic rags almost stifle the adventurous pilgrim with their perfume. The mansion is of primitive construction; simply logs with a dirt roof, but with a taste that evinces true culture. The roof is ornamented with kerosene cans in every stage of dilapidation, while the pleasure grounds adjacent to the house are covered with thousands of bottles—a correct and enduring monument to the dryness of the Hills.

When the reporter arrived at Frenchy's place, he was met by the owner, and the description continues, stating that

the interior of the domicile is perhaps different to any other structure on the face of the earth. A couch of the very finest assorted rags occupied one corner, while the banqueting hall showed the remnants of a feast to which the slop barrels of our hotels had contributed liberally. The Fiend, as he is irreverently called, is descended from an ancient and noble family, but tired of the indolences and debauchery of a corrupt court, he came to a free land where he could gratify his simple tastes in his own manner.[8]

As noted previously, in June 1877 Frenchy won a court settlement against a man named Bill Aylmer after the latter assaulted the Frenchman. The defendant had been found guilty of assault and battery and fined a total of $22. Perhaps the results of those injuries created the odd behavior of Frenchy, the Bottle Fiend. In a March 1878 issue of the *Times*, the editor noted that Deadwood now had four crazy people, three of whom had only recently gone over the edge, "but the Bottle Fiend had been crazy for some time."[9]

A few days later, the *Times* noted again that Frenchy had diversified his collecting habits, and was now also retrieving bottle corks from the gutter. In early April 1878, the *Times* imagined that Frenchy had taken his "annual face bath," a sure harbinger of spring in the Black Hills.[10] By November, though, Frenchy had impressed his neighbors and the city's health workers so much that they had him arrested for maintaining a nuisance in the form of "The Bottle Ranch" (so named because empty bottles were the crop he harvested).

This is the point where the Deadwood legal system gets a bit confusing. Frenchy was hauled off to the town jail, and the judge set his bail at $200. Somehow Frenchy magically produced the money, and went back to City Creek to make the ranch more acceptable to his neighbors and the town in general. The question that begs to be asked more than a century and a quarter later is: If Bill Aylmer inflicted the beating that created Frenchy's craziness, why didn't he have to pay that bail for Frenchy?

Toward the end of May 1878, a local judge decided to examine Frenchy in an attempt to find out just how crazy he was. Frenchy had a long discussion with the judge and, based on the judge's keen knowledge of Black Hills Gold Rush Craziness, His Honor determined that Frenchy had a level head. Be that as it may, the *Times* would get a lot of mileage out of Frenchy during that year of 1878, printing at least twenty-five brief articles and a few longer ones to keep the local readership apprised of the progress of his perceived insanity.

While Frenchy may have been ruled sane by one judge in May, a different judge found that perception completely without merit the following January. Frenchy's Bottle Ranch now provided a home for an estimated 25,000 previously abandoned bottles, and the city thought that was just about enough. In front of this other judge, Frenchy was declared partially insane and shipped to an asylum for rehabilitation.

It now finally dawned on reporters for the *Times* that they were not going to be able to follow Frenchy's antics in the paper for a while, so in protest, they wrote a rather long article about the hobby of collecting, comparing Frenchy's bottle collection to Daniel Webster's famous coin collection and "Mrs. Gen." Winfield Scott's button collection. The article ended with the statement, "If [Frenchy] was mad, surely there was 'method in his madness'."

The fact that Frenchy was no longer in Deadwood was noticed far and wide, and the Leadville, Colorado *Reveille* took it as an omen that the Black Hills were being forsaken, citing "Fanatical Frenchy, the Bottle Fiend, hasn't returned" as one of its proofs.

Frenchy's stay at the asylum was pretty brief, and by mid-March he could be found on the streets of Deadwood again, under the watchful eyes of the *Black Hills Daily Times.* When Frenchy was observed passing by discarded bottles and large cigar butts, only to walk into a store and purchase a package of tobacco, this was duly covered. Within a scant few days it became known that Frenchy was looking for legal assistance. By the end of the month, the *Black Hills Daily Times* announced that Frenchy was suing Lawrence County for the destruction of his personal property when, during his absence, the county incinerated the Bottle Ranch. A sampling of Frenchy's list, as the *Times* jokingly claimed, included such items as:

700 Lbs. Tobacco, assorted, at 50 cts	*350.00*
700,000 corks, assorted, at 1 ct.	*700.00*
13 pair gloves, mouse eaten no fingers 1.00	*13.00*
20 choice self moving cheese	*80.00*
1 bar soap, inexhaustible	*1.00*
37 letters diplomatic correspondence	*100.00*
1 tooth brush and stove brush combination	*1.00*

Following a long list of such items, the *Times* made the first true statement in the article by saying, "It is a well known fact that this individual did more in the way of cleaning the streets and alleys of rubbish during the past year than did the street commissioner, who received a large quantity of county warrants [payment vouchers] for his labor."[11]

So, while the *Times* still chose to poke fun at the Bottle Fiend, its staff very much missed the presence of the old man when he was not on the street.

By the end of June 1879, Frenchy had reverted to his old ways, and was again collecting bottles and old cigar butts. The *Times* recommended that Frenchy be invited to march in the Fourth of July parade, but admitted that they had no idea how to keep him from breaking ranks whenever he spied a bottle or a decent cigar butt. They did suggest that a blindfold might do the trick, but there would be the risk of his stealing the thunder of all the other parade marchers.[12]

In August, a month before the Great Fire, the *Black Hills Daily Times*

A bulwark of innumberable bottles and barrels surrounded Frenchy's modest cabin.

printed a spoof interview with Frenchy: "[W]hen asked yesterday how business in the bottle line was, [he] replied that he had given up beer bottles and was only dealing in wine bottles; that he had on hand about four million, and was indignant when asked if he would sell them by the dozen. He promptly stated that he would sell them only by the [railroad] carload. Pity probate Judge Fraser was not again in power to break up his little scheme."

During Deadwood's Great Fire of 1879, folks fled in several different directions, mostly on foot. Many of them headed to the mining shafts on Hebrew Hill (later Mount Moriah), others ran up Deadwood Creek toward Gayville and Central City, and still more went up City Creek where Frenchy's new cabin was. His Bottle Ranch was one of the last sites on that creek to burn. When asked by the *Times* about his place, he claimed that "his loss was nothing to speak of outside of his business, which had suffered wonderfully."

After the fire, one Deadwood resident wanted to give thanks in a tangible way. Dennis Hannafin, who once had owned the *Bismarck Tribune*, "espying Old Frenchy. . . captured him and marched him into a clothing house" where he purchased "new harness" from hat to shoes for the Bottle

Fiend. Then he gave him money for a bath, haircut, and shave. Frenchy emerged looking dapper in a new bowler hat, suit ("under clothes and all"), plus boots and overcoat.[13]

January 1880 found Frenchy still actively making his rounds, and the *Times* still giving a running account of his activities. "The only scavengers we have in Deadwood are Old Frenchy and the few swine which go rooting and grunting about the streets," noted the paper. "They shall probably be the only ones we shall ever have in the absence of a city organization. Therefore O. F. and the swine should be protected and encouraged."

Frenchy's antics continued to be newsworthy in January and February 1880. Then, in the first week of March, the town experienced a bitter cold snap. The *Times* informed their readership that Frenchy had "frosted" his hands and feet but that he would soon be on the streets again. He was seen hobbling around on crutches.[14] By March 19 it was recognized that Frenchy had been more seriously hurt by that freeze and was now temporarily crippled. He was laid up in his cabin, and efforts were made to get him admitted to the hospital.

Frenchy's former friends at the *Times* ran an article wanting know "why our people should increase their taxes to humor the old nuisance. . . ." This was inspired by the report that Frenchy had wealthy brothers in Nebraska who could care for him. Finally, on the 27th, Judge John Allen ordered that Frenchy be removed from his cabin and taken to "the Sisters' hospital."[15] Hank Beaman was one of the men who carried out that order, and this was his report: "He lay there in a bed, filthy and almost in a putrefying condition, without care, food or fire. The chances are that the old unfortunate will never recover, and if he should he will be a cripple for life."

Naturally, after the fact, the *Times* called for Frenchy to be saved, saying "Why not send him to the hospital until he recovers? Charity reaches all cases." How quickly the winds change. While Frenchy was in the hospital, interlopers began to appear on the scene. In April, . . . "an eccentric individual has started a little junk shop opposite Wertheimer's Hall. He buys old iron, rags and everything valuable; his boys cart the iron to the foundry for sale and the rags are shipped east. He will beat old Frenchy in rooting out scraps, iron, old gunny sacks, etc."

The following day, the *Black Hills Daily Times* reported: "There is another bottle fiend in the field. He is located below Chinatown at Bob Howe's bakery. He is a young man and pays ten cents a dozen for beer bottles."

The year 1880 was when Pat Early became seriously involved with bottles. Mr. Early had been elected to the post of Street Commissioner, and he began a serious campaign to rid the streets of bottles and other trash. With no municipal area for disposing of the trash, the yard surrounding Early's home on Sherman Street began to look a lot like Frenchy's Bottle Ranch. But where Frenchy's collection had grown out of sight; Early's assemblage was in plain view, right in town. Thus, Deadwood had to begin a concerted effort to clean up the act of the street cleaner, threatening Early with fines and jail. The implication was obvious—whether they knew it or not, Deadwood needed a Frenchy, and not just for comic relief.

In June, Frenchy was out of the hospital, but he never moved quite the same way again, and perhaps out of kindness the *Times* stopped following his life. Then in November 1880 there was this small page-four mention: "Old Frenchy slipped and fell down the five step offset in the sidewalk in front of the Minnesota Bakery on Sherman street and it is feared that he may be seriously injured." At the very least, he fractured three of his ribs.

Frenchy was taken back home, and again left on his own. Several days later two Good Samaritans decided to check on him. As before, he was discovered "in his cabin on City Creek in a most filthy and deplorable condition." The men procured a sled and hauled him into Deadwood for care.

There a *Times* reporter visited "Justin Cachlin," as the article was respectfully headlined, in a convalescent hospital on December 6, finding him alert and responsive, still receiving treatment for "the wound in his side," which dated from nine months previously. Not to mention that Cachlin had good food, general cleanliness, warmth, and support from "the good shepherdess" Mrs. Burnham, whose frequently charitable hospital it was.[16]

Nevertheless, the *Black Hills Evening Press* shortly announced that Old Frenchy had died, and ran a half-column obituary. The essence of the *Press* article was that the man was in fact little more than an animal, a "demented, driveling creature—a bugbear and a terror to timid children."

In an unprecedented collaboration, the *Times* and the *Pioneer* both wrote rebuttals to the *Press* article. The *Times*' response was that Frenchy was indeed "peculiar, yet we never heard of him doing a mean or wicked act. He was never a beggar and never violated any of our laws. When spoken to he always gave a courteous and intelligent answer. And . . . he is not dead, or was not at dark last evening, and we hope he may recover and again perambulate the streets of Deadwood, and settle with his biographer in cigar stumps."

The *Pioneer* joined in by saying that one more dose of the *Evening Press* would be fatal to poor Frenchy.

Then the *Evening Press* story was picked up by the *Bismarck Tribune*, which further spread the word: "Frenchy, the well known bottle fiend of the Hills, is dead."[17] When the very much alive Frenchy was asked at the hospital if the *Press* had succeeded in killing him, he replied "Am I a match to be broken in two?"

What the readership of Deadwood did not know was that Frenchy had been slowly declining, and then he truly died at 6 A.M. on December 23, 1880. The *Pioneer* wrote a compassionate obituary the following day, which was followed by a *Times* article on Frenchy's problems with the *Evening Press*. The article ended with a prediction that the *Press*, like the little boy who always cried wolf, "would be eaten up someday soon by public contempt."

After the turn of the year, the *Times* ran a mournful poem concerning Frenchy's demise.[18]

Lines of the Death of Old Frenchy

He tramped through the streets of our city,
And he begged for our castaway bread,
With castaway cloth[e]s on his body,
And a castaway hat on his head.

What though he were shot in the battle,
Where he fought for our flag while he bled:
He was only a county pauper,
And who weeps for a pauper dead?

They bore him high on the mountain,
And there they dug him a mean shallow tomb;
He was only a county pauper,
And his death brought to nobody gloom.

Far away from the land of his birth;
Far away from the graves of his dead,
At his grave not a prayer was uttered—
Not a pitying tear was there shed.

Has old age no claim to man's pity[,]
To a pauper will none be a friend?
What if the hopes and dreams of your youth
Should, in old age, in such misery end?

When your brow is furrowed and wrinkled,
If you die in the old pauper's lot;
Then you, like the pauper "Old Frenchy,"
Will be left on the mountain to rot.

By May 1881, Deadwood's streets, sidewalks, and paths were littered with thousands of bottles and millions of pieces of broken glass. The front and back doors of all the saloons were crowded with refuse, "and all wished the old man back." Things got so desperate that Molitor, the assayer, proposed using bottles to build business buildings and municipal structures, claiming that because of their design, bottles could stand significant amounts of weight and would be ideal building materials for structures up to five stories high.

Meanwhile, Street Commissioner Patrick Early was trying desperately to keep ahead of the growing bottle population by storing wagonloads of them in a gulch just outside of town. Early's plan was to hide them there until the railroad arrived and then ship them back east, making his fortune. He didn't realize just how long he would be waiting for that train (a narrow-gauge railroad for ore from the mines finally began puffing in 1888, but no full-gauge line ever arrived), while his bottle gulch grew exponentially.

In February 1882, the ire of Deadwoodites rose to an unprecedented level when the *Bismarck Tribune* ran a long article recommending the bones of Wild Bill Hickok be removed from Deadwood and taken to the Smithsonian Institution! The *Times* ran a scathing rebuttal that claimed Wild Bill's bones were as much of a Black Hills institution as the Whiterocks or "Frenchy's bottle pile." In November the final reference to Frenchy ran in the *Times*, when they noted: "In front of the Minnesota [Bakery] a man-trap exists that should have been taken care of years ago, as it was at that very place that 'Old Frenchy' fell on Thanksgiving day of 1880, and received injuries which resulted in his death."[19]

HENRICO LIVINGSTONE: OBSTRUCTIONIST EXTRAORDINAIRE

"You wild children get off my land! Run right back into the schoolyard where you belong!" The tall fortune-teller grabbed stones, and lobbed them at the pint-sized claim jumpers, reinforcing her demand. The fury of Madame Henrico arose once again.

Perhaps one of the most colorful non-sporting ladies to live in Deadwood in its earliest years was Madame Henrico Livingstone, yet she has been surprisingly unsung. In Deadwood's usual histories, the lady barely rates a page; Robert Casey's 1949 work mentioned her in passing, but from what he wrote we believe he did not know her story.[1]

That the lady was colorful is clear in Estelline Bennett's memoir of her childhood, including her experience with Henrico:

> *She had an unpleasant habit of throwing stones at the school children who strayed out of the school yard which backed up from Main Street. I suppose she thought we wanted to jump her claim.*

The boys entered gaily into the stone throwing with the result that Miss Livingstone, a tall, grim figure, shabby, stiff and dour, would stalk into the school room to lay her grievances before the principal.[2]

Estelline remarked on the phenomenon one day to her father, Judge Granville Bennett, who told her he had never heard of Henrico coming into the school yard to throw stones, and that school children had no business in her yard. He also said his own children should have no occasion to ever walk on the road in front of her yard.

In January 1842, Henrico was born to English parents on a ship bound for Maryland in the United States.[3] Little is known about her youth except that she married young in Indiana or Illinois, where she and her husband ran or worked for a detective agency. It was in this line of work that Henrico first began wearing men's clothing for undercover work. Her tall, slender build was a natural for such disguises.

When the Civil War broke out, Henrico's husband enlisted and, because of his previous experience, was given the rank of regiment captain. Henrico again donned men's clothing and enlisted in his regiment, where she served a greater part of a four-year enlistment.[4] After the war, which her husband apparently did not survive, Henrico followed the gold camps of Colorado, telling fortunes to make a living, before moving north to Deadwood.[5]

Arriving in Deadwood as early as July 1877, Madame Henrico Livingstone purchased a town lot on the north side of the Gayville toll road, near City Creek. The hill where her house stood was subsequently known as Livingstone Hill. In early August, she was advertising her services as a fortune-teller and "medical clairvoyant," using her City Creek home as her primary place of business.[6] In December of that same year, she had hosted a most enjoyable social party.[7] So, in Deadwood's early days, the tall, slender lady was not recognized as being any crazier, ornerier, or meaner than the rest of the population.

Henrico's real problems did not begin until she decided to patent a mining claim on Livingstone Hill. In October 1882, she applied for a patent, and the application was posted in the newspaper on three different occasions over the next ninety days. In March 1883, Henrico received a

CHOICEST BRANDS OF

LIQUORS, WINES, & CIGARS

The Proprietors, Schuchart & Ludwig with Mr. Spencer, have opened the

SENATE SALOON IN CENTRAL

It is in full blast and is doing a rushing business
Drop in for an hour in the evening and
listen to the Music by the Band
and regale yourself on a

Refreshing Glass of Beer

From the Black Hills Brewery, Deadwood.

SPENCER SCHUCHART & LUDWIG, Proprs.

KNOW THY DESTINY.

MADAME HENRICO,

Medical Clairvoyant, and Fortune Teller
Toll road to Gayville, one hundred yards south
of City Creek, Deadwood. See sign.

"Madame Henrico" advertised her services as a "medical clairvoyant," doing business out of her home in Deadwood.

patent for the claim she called the "Harry Livingstone Lode." The major flaw in the patent was a small clause protecting the surface rights to deeded townsite lots that were within the boundaries of her claim. Henrico felt that the patent was practically worthless without the surface rights, so she set about to secure possession of the surface.[8] Not to be deterred by such trifles as viability, she acquired several adjoining claims also.[9]

In June 1883, Father Peter Rosen of the Catholic Church, which was positioned directly south of Henrico's claim, decided that he needed a new stable behind the church. He hired an elderly German man to grade the area to use as a foundation. After showing the man where he wanted his stable, Father Rosen let the work begin. That is when Henrico began protesting that the property, and the mineral values therein, belonged to her. And she accused the priest and his worker of trespassing. She successfully ran the suspected trespassers off her property, only to have them press charges against her for assault. After several days in court, she was found guilty. The judge fined her $5 and costs, a verdict for which Henrico immediately gave notice of appeal. By August, Father Rosen must have felt that all the ruffled feathers had been smoothed; he rehired men to resume work on his stable and immediately ran into more opposition from Madame Henrico. Once again Henrico was hauled in front of a judge for assault, once again pleading not guilty, and once again losing her case.[10]

The years of 1884 and 1885 must have been far too uneventful for the editors of the *Pioneer*, and for the most part they were certainly calmer than the years before Henrico first appeared in the news. That is, until the *Pioneer* decided to publish the following note:

> *Mrs. Henrico Livingstone staked out a mill site on the hill just below the reservoirs that contain the city's water supply. She will use the water from the north tanks to run the mill.*[11]

One can only imagine the controversy created by that brief note. But Henrico was up to the chore, and after she wearied of the din she launched the following rebuttal in the *Times*:

> *Caution. To whom it may concern. The statement in the Deadwood* Pioneer *of Sept. 3d, 1885, to the effect that I have staked a mill site over or about the city water works is false, and if any such location has been made in my name, I hereby forbid all persons buying or selling the same, and if any sale has been made of the property located in my name, the sale is illegal. Henrico L. Livingstone.*[12]

If Henrico was relatively sedate during the years 1884 and 1885, it might be because she was deep in thought over what she planned for 1886. She started the year by addressing the city's Common Council, asking why her property was being taxed, "inasmuch as although it is all mining property, she is not permitted to work it, as all water is taken from City Creek to supply the city reservoirs." The Common Council referred her to the committee on mining roads and prospective sidewalks, in an obvious effort to sidestep the question.[13]

Perhaps their maneuver enlightened Henrico as to the city's plans to extend a thoroughfare across her claim, because she was ready when they arrived. Well armed and waiting at her property line, Henrico faced the vicious hoards. As might be suspected, Henrico was again subdued, taken to jail, and then indicted for malicious mischief by a grand jury. While she was in court, the judge told her that he was not ready to hear her case and he set bail at $0 and stated that she was free on her own recognizance. To this she answered that she had a right to go to jail, stating that once a Mrs. Lovell was freed on her own recognizance and was subsequently robbed and murdered. She carefully explained to the judge that she did not want to be robbed and murdered, so she would go to jail. The sheriff and a small group of other men attempted to change her mind, but she steadfastly refused to listen to them, so she was taken to jail.[14]

The next day, the *Times* announced that Henrico had taken up permanent quarters at the county jail. They described how she had gone to her house to obtain her bedding and clothing, and was "arranging her apartment for a comfortable sojourn." She lost the case again, and was eventually extracted from her comfortable hermitage in the jail to fend for herself as well as possible.[15]

Even in a small town there are always those who never seem to get the news. In May 1886, it was the phone company. Problems were reported with the line between Deadwood and Gayville. So workers were dispatched to Livingstone Hill. Ben Garr and his assistant were in the cross-trees of a telephone pole on Henrico's claim, repairing the line when Henrico approached them, heavily armed. "With no uncertain language she ordered the linemen to descend and decamp, both men complied."[16] The newspapers leave us with little evidence of the result, perhaps because it was a repetition of old news for the Deadwood readership.

Henrico's house stood above the Gayville Road, near City Creek, on what became known as Livingstone Hill. COURTESY DEADWOOD HISTORY, INC., DEADWOOD, SD.

In September, Henrico had the following "unofficial" paper drawn up, and served it on City Creek resident Joseph Girard:

> *You are hereby warned to desist from excavating, building or in any other manner encumbering or trespassing upon the Rose and Harry Livingstone Quartz lodes, and all other lands and lodes worked by me. You have been a trespasser upon my mining claims for many years and thereby aided in preventing mining operations and mineral development; therefore you are hereby notified to remove from my mining claims within thirty days from the date hereof, as the ground you occupy is required for mining purposes.*

When the *Times* editor picked up on Henrico's activities regarding a long-time resident with a city lot ownership deed, the text hit the fan, in a manner of speaking. He sent a plea out for some sort of legal intervention, calling Henrico "a great annoyance, not to say a nuisance to many property owners and to city officials, harassing them with notes and notices and not infrequently personal abuse."[17]

The article ended on an ominous note, stating that "Henrico should take a tumble." As a grand culmination to 1886, in October Henrico found herself in court again, but this time it was for a sanity hearing. The public normally followed this sort of proceeding very closely, but this time there was little to follow because nothing was published in the *Times*. This must have meant they could not cart her off to the asylum in Yankton.[18]

In May 1887, interpretation of the war shifted from Henrico the community nuisance to Henrico the miner versus the General Land Office. As trying as Henrico may have been to the city fathers, Livingstone Hill residents, and anyone trying to accomplish any kind of work near her mineral claims, the mining community rushed in for clarification when the Land Office served Henrico with papers recalling her patent on the Harry Livingstone Lode. Such a move on the federal government's part threatened the safety of all surface mineral claimants in the gulch. Area miners began to circulate a petition asking the Land Commissioner to reopen the case and hold a rehearing, which many signed and forwarded to the commission. Thus what at first appeared to be a miracle for the city commission and the road crews backlashed and became a movement of irate miners.[19]

This should have filled Henrico with joy, but on further examination it became clear that a large number of Deadwood inhabitants had also filed a petition claiming that Henrico's mining claim was without precious-metals value, but was exceedingly valuable for municipal purposes. Thus the patent was being held for cancellation.[20] As might be expected, Henrico promptly put everything on hold by filing an appeal.[21]

By April 1888, the General Land Office had not attended to Henrico's appeal, so when the city decided to make road improvements where Williams Street crosses the City Creek Bridge, Henrico was on hand for the event. She approached the road crew with a very ugly hatchet and everything came to a halt while a worker ran off to fetch Marshal Dunn. The marshal arrived, evaluated the situation and arrested Henrico who, while not exactly willing, accompanied him to jail.[22] Henrico was arraigned before Judge Hall for disorderly conduct (though some thought she should be arraigned on charges of assault). Judge Hall was more than willing to allow Henrico to go her own way if she would promise not to molest or interfere with the road graders. She vehemently declined to do so, and was escorted back to her cell.[23]

After Henrico had spent a week in jail, the *Times* informed its news-hungry readership that Henrico was occupying a "cozy cell" and would remain there until the Williams Street road improvements were completed.[24] Less than a week after she was released from jail, Henrico was arrested again for threatening road-crew workers on Williams Street. Henrico must have had advance warning that they were coming because she was ready to greet them on arrival. Once again, she was off to jail and court where she refused to post bond or promise not to interfere. So she sat in jail again.[25]

It is difficult to understand how the human mind works, and often there is no logical explanation for a person's behavior. On October 5, 1889, after more than a year of silence, Henrico walked to Lead, where she met Father Metzger of the Catholic Church and offered to sign over all of her mining claims to her old nemesis, the church. In the final paperwork she asked for no considerations except a proviso that required the recipients to faithfully perform the annual assessment work on each of the five claims until full title was secured from the Land Office.[26]

A month following Henrico's deed of gift to the Catholic Church, the General Land Office ruled against Henrico's claim appeal of 1887, which she now appealed to the Secretary of the Interior. This thrust Henrico back into a position where she felt she needed to protect her property rights, much to the dissatisfaction of concerned Deadwood residents.[27] Surprisingly, though, it was actually the harbinger of a period of relative peace and quiet, and an uneasy silence settled across the Livingstone Hill war zone.

Toward the end of July 1891, the city of Deadwood again let a contract for improving Williams Street, which included that portion of the street that passed through Henrico's mining claims. Henrico put on her shawl and walked to Central City. There she pressed charges against Deadwood's Mayor, Sol Star, and the entire City Council, contractors, and a road gang for conspiring to deprive her by fraud and stealth of her rights in the Rose mining claim.[28] The officials were all promptly arrested but then released when the judge ruled that all they were trying to do was make repairs to Williams Street.[29] Henrico was incensed. Returning home, she set up camp at the site of the proposed road improvements and waited for the morning road crew to arrive. When they did, she promptly filed charges again; the road crew was arrested, taken to Central City and then released when they appeared in front of the judge requesting a dismissal.[30]

Previously, Henrico had been merely annoyed that the legal system was paying her no mind, but she now became electrified by the situation. With her tobacco-can lunch pail and an iron bar, she set up camp on the road crew's waste dirt pile and waited. Upon their arrival, she warned them to "meander forth only upon pain of death." The construction boss immediately sent men to fetch the city marshal. The current office holder, Marshal Garr, returned with a deputy and, after some difficulty, arrested her. At the time, she brandished an iron bar in one hand and the metal lunch pail in the other. An examination of the pail produced a pipe and a package of tobacco, a few odds and ends of minimal comforts, and a dangerous-looking Bulldog revolver. Henrico was once again hauled off to jail.[31]

The next morning, Marshal Garr escorted Henrico into court. She was arraigned on charges of wholesale threats against life, limb, and liberty of the men working on the Williams Street improvements. Henrico's only response was to request a postponement and to demand a jury trial, all of which Justice Stannus granted.[32] In this case, Judge Bennett represented the state, and he was quick to point out that Stannus's court did not have jurisdiction to determine the defendant's guilt or innocence, but only to determine if there was sufficient guilt to hold the accused for the grand jury.

Justice Stannus ruled in favor of Henrico, and a previously sworn jury filed into the box. Judge Bennett stood and stated that the proceedings were so unusual that he confessed ignorance of how to conduct the case further. Bennett then stormed out of the courtroom. Justice Stannus then declared that the state had failed to prove their case for want of prosecution and subsequently discharged Henrico. He then signed $2 certificates as compensation for each of the twelve jurymen. There seemed to be some doubt among the spectators who frequented the street corners and saloons that the county would honor the certificates.[33]

Henrico must have taken this as divine intervention and an invitation to retire from the position of property-rights advocate because it is the last recorded brush she had with the law. At fifty years of age, the rigors of mining life were beginning to catch up with Henrico, and her tall, thin body was beginning to bow. She became a common figure as she went about town visiting this person and that, telling romantic stories of her life, and selling the occasional small item.

One of Henrico's primary economic survival strategies was "the Raffle." Wearing a much-faded gray suit with a shawl to cover her head, she carried a small brown satchel that she hinted held her most important papers. From the satchel she showed her potential customers the raffle prize—a nice watch—enticing them to purchase raffle tickets. Somehow, over the years, the watch was never won and remained in her possession.

During the course of her life, Henrico did not once accept charity, and she never considered going to the poor house. On January 12, 1910, Henrico slipped into a coma.[34] Surrounded by well-wishers and despite voluntary medical aid, she failed to regain consciousness. Henrico's obituary ran in newspapers across the nation, but for all the notoriety there was no money for a proper burial. She was buried in an unmarked grave on Mount Moriah.

GENERAL SAMUEL FIELDS: POLITICAL ASPIRANT

Sam Fields really believed in participatory democracy, and he loved elections, as a candidate and, especially, as a soapbox orator. In Deadwood, he found his life's greatest success as a business owner, even though folks laughed at his political aspirations.

Perhaps one of the most colorful and fascinating individuals to not grace the annals of Western America's history was Samuel F. Fields, frequently called, in the repugnant slang of the day, "the Nigger General," who moved around the central United States during the time of Black Hills gold hysteria. Fields settled in Deadwood for a decade before moving on to less tumultuous digs in Omaha, but he left an indelible mark on Black Hills history. In the process of his occupation (a general usually occupies the lands he has captured), he earned such titles as the Shakespearian Darky and the Colored Orator of Omaha, along with a plethora of degrading and racial slurs. Amazingly though, through his many trials and tribulations, he appears to have left this life without ever having done physical harm to a single person.

Fields was born a free black person in April 1849 in Louisiana. His father had been born in Illinois and his mother in Virginia.[1] Fields worked his father's farm until he was fourteen years of age, when he joined the United States Colored Troops, or Corps D'Afrique, on October 12, 1863, in New Orleans. He was mustered into the 4th Cavalry on the 27th as a private with a monthly pay rate of $7. His military record was unblemished except for the loss of a spur and a leather strap, an expense the army deducted from his pay. On March 20, 1866, when he was mustered out of the cavalry in New Orleans, he was due a total of $31.72.[2] In 1870 the United States census noted he was living in Raceland, Louisiana, working as a farm laborer.[3]

After leading an exciting life in the cavalry, living on a rural southern farm probably did not appeal much to Fields, who started working his way west in the early 1870s. He first found employment in Omaha, at the Herndon Hotel. During the Civil War, he had visited that city, and it apparently left a positive memory.[4] From Omaha, he traveled to Denver as early as January 1874.

In his debut in the Denver press, Fields was noted as being the chaplain of the "Third House" independent political party. Published as what appears to be a rather lengthy parody, the article in all probability referred to an actual event.

> *General Samuel Fields, the colored chaplain, was induced to give his political views as bearing on legislative Matters. He cut quite a comical figure and excited much merriment, especially when he assured his hearers that he expected to enter the doors of the next legislature.*

This article also provides the earliest known instance of Fields' being referred to as the "General," as well as his entry into the political arena.[5] Several Colorado newspapers covered the same event with similarly mocking articles.

In September 1874, Denver newspapers began a series of articles on the local election campaigns. The first, concerned a meeting to discuss Colorado politics and possible statehood. The main speaker, General Chamberlain, stated that he did not care if Governor Evans and his running mate, Joe Chaffee, were elected as senators, or if the winners were

Without corroborating evidence it cannot be confirmed, but this image may be that of Samuel Fields during his time in Deadwood.

their opponents, General Fields and Mr. Lowry. This article was of a serious nature and did not even hint of humor.[6]

The next day an article ran, supposedly signed by Fields, announcing himself as an independent candidate for Congress. Stating that he was running as the "Blooded Candidate" (meaning he was a Civil War battlefield veteran, a point of honor), he supposedly said, "I cannot be coaxed off the track, although I may be bought."[7]

An article covering a speech from candidate Lowery states that a call for General Fields to speak interrupted him. Fields had been busy lighting all the lamps in the hall, and he told the crowd to let the gentleman (Mr. Lowery) finish and then he (Fields) would be glad to speak. When Lowery finished, Fields took the stump and made some pretty strong points before telling the audience that "he would be going to Washington even if he had to go afoot." On that note, the hall erupted with laughter and applause, and the meeting adjourned.[8]

During the first week of September, Fields' name appeared in the local newspapers no fewer than nine times. In most cases, it was blatantly obvious that the press thought of the whole affair as a joke, and Fields' campaign something of a minstrel show. In retrospect, however, what is not obvious is how Fields may have felt about it. It is likely that he viewed himself as a serious candidate on this and several future occasions. But when Denver newspapers published the election results of 1874, Fields was not even mentioned as a participant or a contender.

In January 1875, Fields was referred to as the "late [recent] independent candidate for delegate to congress." For all intents, it appears the primary focus of the article was the amusement of the newspaper's white readers more than an actual dissemination of meaningful news. The column quickly digressed to covering a totally unrelated subject, an altercation Fields had had with a man named Johnny Lingo (also African American). Lingo fell out with Fields and allegedly threatened his life.

> *The General, not fancying the idea of being hustled out of this world without so much as settling his business, much less attending to spiritual wants, swore out a warrant and placed it in Constable Force'[s] hands, and last night Lingo was in a fair way to change base to limbo.*[9]

Police arrested Fields on a charge of larceny the following month. The *Denver News* declared the case to be dreadfully repulsive. Fields and another man, Pete Smith, described as "darkies as black as the ace of spades," were arrested for the alleged theft of some bed clothing and undisclosed other items. Perhaps the real crime was the fact that Fields, now in his mid-twenties, was living with a young German girl. The article did not give her name, but said she came from a respectable family. She was held in jail on $100 bail as a witness against Fields and Smith. The men were held on $200 bail each.[10] In April, Smith was released due to a lack of evidence, but the indictment against Fields stood. A disclaimer at the end of the article indicated that a number of people had "skipped" bail. This might have been an indication that Fields had already left the Denver area for friendlier digs, because the media mentioned nothing more about this affair or any trial.[11]

From Denver, Fields followed the gold excitement to Cheyenne in Wyoming Territory, where he purportedly joined the party of Colonel Steele and Judge Kuykendall heading for the Black Hills. In his book, *Frontier Days*, Kuykendall wrote that he found it surprising that Fields was a Democrat, because Lincoln, the Great Emancipator, had been a Republican.[12] The Kuykendall party made its way to the Black Hills early in the spring of 1876, but somehow Fields seems to have missed the trek—or did he?

July 1876 found General Samuel Fields on 16th Street in Cheyenne, giving a speech on his opinions about "the Indian Question" to a surprised group of European dignitaries who by chance fell into his clutches. While the Europeans were quite taken by the general's oratorical skills, the locals were not, and they proceeded to drive him off the street in a hail of rotten eggs. To say that Fields found Cheyenne to be somewhat less receptive to his ways than Denver had been would be a considerable understatement. One of the two articles in the *Cheyenne Daily Leader* about his speech on Indian policy started with slurs and threatening language: "Gen. Sam Fields, a disreputable nigger who should be driven out of Wyoming. . . ."[13]

So, did Fields arrive in Deadwood with Kuykendall's party and then turn right around to repeat the sixty-hour trip back south to Cheyenne? Here's the problem: Only ten days before this event, Pete Smith, the butcher across the street from the Welch House, observed Fields in Deadwood.

Always starved for news, no matter how trivial, the *Pioneer* reported that Fields was the thief who had stolen a sprinkler.

Sprinkler? As the story goes, around daybreak on the 12th a butcher standing in front of his shop observed a white man on the other side of the street with a water sprinkler (to help mop wooden floors) and a tin pail full of whiskey. Whenever the man met someone along his way, he would stop them and offer them a drink from the pail. Growing weary of such fun, he set the sprinkler down, and continued on his way with just the pail of whiskey. A short time later the General happened along and recovered the sprinkler as though he had been looking for it. The curious butcher wanted to know from the *Pioneer* if the General had taken new employment as a saloon cleaner.

Employed or not, the remarkable speed of Fields' supposed trip to Cheyenne and back again might qualify him for work in a far different field—magic.[14] Perhaps, by the time Judge Kuykendall wrote his book, he'd forgotten exactly where he and Sam Fields discussed politics.

Fields had a grand command of the English language and thought of himself as a great tragedian, and his talents shined on the streets of Deadwood, where people often referred to him as the "Shakespearian Darkie."[15] But the federal census of 1900 noted that Fields could not read or write. Whether this was an assumption made by a careless census taker or a fact may never be known. Fields' entry in the 1870 Louisiana census had indicated that he could not write but could read English.[16] In that era of memorizing and speaking "pieces," and of groups reading aloud on long winter evenings, even the semi- or non-literate were exposed to the vocabularies and sentence structures of the King James Bible, poetry, Shakespeare, and other works of literature.

The best example of Fields' oratorical style has come down to us in an article that covers a speech Fields made in Cheyenne in 1876. What follows is a brief excerpt:

> *Fellow Citizen, I rise before this isolated assembly to concus the ethereal and indivisible subjects of the Sheyen in Wyoming which are reciting the minds of the hieroglyphic public in regard to the Black Hills and the Deadwood at the present time. (Prolonged*

applause) The occidental and contaminating cries of disunionism and Indian murders in the Red Canyon are being hurled with rejestic vigor from one end of this elaborate and pusillanimous nation to the other. (Cries of "go take a drink").

The speech goes on for some time, but is finally disrupted when someone in the audience produced a bag of stolen potatoes and began throwing them at Fields. One hundred and thirty-some years later, we are left to wonder how much the speech was altered by the "unbiased" press for entertainment purposes, pure orneriness, and a representation of Fields' propensity for strong drink. Even at a casual glance, it seems that Samuel Fields was someone the folks in the "New West" were unprepared for.[17]

Here is a place to discuss the perceived social environment of Deadwood during this period. "Nigger Hill and Gulch" mining district is located near Deadwood. The name is rather fluid, in that it seems to change in newsprint based on the mood of the reporter, author or observer. One day it would be called "African Gulch," then in a follow-up article it would be "Negro Gulch," and by the end of the week it was back to being "Nigger Gulch."

The hill, gulch, and creek have the distinction of being named after "four gemmen of color" who had discovered rich placer claims about fifteen miles west of Deadwood in 1876. The men took out $75,000 worth of gold, then became afraid that they might end up the victims of an assassin's knife blade. The fear became so horrific that they finally sold off their claims for a mere $3,000. In all fairness, it needs to be mentioned that other problems existed with the Nigger Hill/Gulch claims, such as an extreme lack of water. The white miners soon discovered they were able to work the claims only a few hours a day because of the water shortage. Even under such natural constraints the white miners still managed to retrieve over $100,000 in 1877.

It is possible that racial tension was the cause of the African Americans selling off their claim. Yet there were black people who were esteemed in the Deadwood community—such as Lucretia "Aunt Lou" Marchbanks and Sarah "Aunt Sally" Campbell. For the most part, however, the respected blacks were women involved in domestic services. There was not a man in the group.[18]

General Fields had a pretty good year in 1877 also; he had come into the possession of several city lots on Williams Street, then turned them around by selling them to Max Fishel for the tidy sum of eighty dollars.[19] Fishel was a tobacco and cigar dealer who found a steady outlet for his products in Deadwood. He would suffer considerable losses during the great fire of 1879, but his profits were significant enough for him to replace his old store with a new brick and fireproof building built to his design.

General Fields appears to have had the market cornered on how to be at the wrong place at the wrong time. When the prominent local mine owner William Gay became jealous of his wife's speaking to other men, he shot and killed one. The young man, Lloyd Forbes, also of Gayville, had given a note to Fields and asked that it be delivered to Mrs. Gay. The note read "Mrs. Gay—Darling—Meet me tonight, by the moonlight." Fields accomplished the delivery.

Mrs. Gay immediately showed the note to her husband, who became infuriated, demanding to know who delivered the note, and then proceeded to ride posthaste after Fields, who by then was halfway back to Deadwood. Gay stopped Fields and threatened him with bodily harm if he did not tell him who the author of the note was. Occasionally prudent, Fields spilled the beans. Gay promptly returned to Gayville, where he found and shot Forbes. During the investigation, it was stated with raised eyebrows that Fields had carried the note between the lovers and tipped off Bill Gay. So, along with Bill Gay, officers also captured the General and held him as a material witness.[20]

During the period of Fields' incarceration as a witness for the Gayville murder case, the *Times* published the story of another man, William Smith of Crook City, who was being held as a witness to a different and unrelated murder. On Smith's arrival, he queried the other inmates about the various reasons they were all in jail and how long they had been incarcerated. When he came to Bill Gay, Gay admitted only to being a witness, and he had been there about nine months. Smith asked several other inmates the same question, getting similar answers from all of them. Feeling rather dispirited, he looked over at Fields and said "What's the nigger in for?" To which Gay responded with, "Oh, he murdered a man." Then Smith sighed,

"The Hell! Got to be locked up with nigger murder[er]s just because we are witnesses!" With that, Smith went looking for the sheriff to try to find a remedy to the situation. We can only assume Bill Gay and the other inmates had a good laugh about it.[21]

Toward the end of Fields' incarceration as state's witness against Bill Gay, the *Pioneer* noted that his testimony would in fact be instrumental in the possible conviction of Gay, a local favorite, and asked the public "what is to be done with the Darkey, General Fields, who has been languishing in the county bastile?" They were of the opinion that he should have to receive a little of the "sauce" that he was dishing up for Bill Gay. The following day the *Times* noted "the General" had been turned loose from his stint in protective custody, and they suggested a solution to the *Pioneer*'s Darkey problem, asking their readership if it wouldn't be to the camp's benefit to run him out of town.[22]

A scant eighteen months later, when Deadwood's first public school teacher was murdered in her sleep, rumors circulated that Fields had been seen outside her home that same night. To further complicate things, Officer Siever noted that the footprints in the teacher's yard were the same size as General Fields'.[23] The local newspapers did nothing to shake the notion of Fields' guilt when they published a short, terse quote from one of the local citizens to the effect that any white woman (meaning the late school marm, Minnie Callison) who "entertains Niggers and Chinamen" deserved to die.[24] When the teacher's husband was asked who he thought might have killed his wife, he also placed the blame on the General. Thus, Fields was back in jail again. This time it was Fields who requested jail for protection, fearing the wrath of a drunken lynch mob. Of course, the *Times* had to step up to the plate and say, "he is a bad Negro and should be given just thirty minutes to skip camp."[25] It was "For his own good."[26]

The General seemed to have a good heart. He was noted as participating in all the functions of Deadwood's black community. At political meetings among Deadwood's African Americans, he was always available to stand on the soapbox for this cause or that.[27] By 1880, Fields had achieved the American dream when he was able to purchase a home next to Hussey's Stables.[28] He even prevented a woman from committing suicide.

But Fields' principal problem, being such a prominent figure, was that he seemed to attract the wrong sort of attention.[29] No matter what he said, it was repeated out of context or rearranged for the entertainment of the newspaper editors and the public at large. When a twister touched down in the gulch, someone said that it was a "hurricane;" the General corrected them, explaining that it was a "cyclone." When the statement was printed in the *Times*, his term became a "Sly-Coon."[30] Several times Fields was arrested for stealing, but there is no record of the cases going to trial in Deadwood for that particular sin.[31]

When it came to intercultural relationships, there is really no evidence of Fields mingling with the Chinese or of their opinion of him, but there was a remarkable note published in early 1882 concerning the reactions of a group of Native Americans to him. The ever-vigilant observers from the *Times* stated that a group of Indians passing Fields on the street presented him with a salute worthy of a monarch. The Indians got closer to Fields and with "mock" seriousness removed their head coverings and bowed almost to the ground. They then faced and advanced with uncovered heads and shook hands with him. The General uncovered his head and returned their respectful gesture.[32]

In April 1882, Fields decided to make a public display of his often-rumored athletic prowess. Filled to the brim with what was described as cheap whiskey or "budge," Fields challenged a man who owned a white cayuse to a public race on Main Street—man against horse. The animal's owner was immensely amused at the idea and immediately started making wagers. Field, stripped to the waist, and drunk as a lord when the race began, ran first up Main Street and then back down. On both legs of the journey, Fields was without a doubt the triumphant sprinter. The owner of the horse cried foul, but for once, the *Times* stood firmly by the General, calling the horseman "white trash," and stating that the General was a runner from way back.[33]

By the end of 1882, Deadwood appears to have grown tired of using the word "nigger" when referring to Fields, and from then on he was most frequently called "General Fields" by the *Black Hills Daily Times*. Does this mean that Deadwood was trying to take some of the edge off its literary racial sword? Or, perhaps, as out in the public as Fields seemed to have constantly been, someone finally noticed that he was a real person. And that real person appeared to be planning to stay for dinner and longer.

Initially, the average man must have felt at a certain disadvantage when confronted with Fields; here was this tall, light brown, handsome man with a superb command of the English language. He mixed well with his own people and wanted to be in charge. He thought he had significant things to say and would not be deterred by the riffraff. In 1883, when the black community held their annual emancipation celebration, Fields was chosen to be the grand marshal; "his splendid horsemanship, military bearing and general excellent appearance was the theme of much favorable comment."[34] In addition to being a skilled equestrian, there is pretty firm evidence that Fields was a dog lover and owner. In the spring of 1883, the *Times* published a brief, curt note on the subject, stating that everyone knew being bitten by a spitz dog would result in hydrophobia (the common term for rabies)! The management at the *Times* sincerely hoped Fields would soon be bitten by his own dog.[35]

While the *Times* was busy praying for a dog bite, the *Pioneer* advertised the opening of General Fields' new chop house on Main Street, called the "Little Fort Meade Palace Restaurant." He guaranteed first class service and satisfaction to all, meals at all times of the day or night, with the greatest luxury the market afforded.[36]

In December 1883, the first electric lights were turned on in Deadwood. While most of the camp's residents had seen the miracle of electricity before, the *Times* reporter had not, stating that because he had been "raised in a sugar trough in the backwoods," he was duly amazed. General Fields stated that he had seen them before the war in New Orleans (where he could have seen oil streetlamps), but had thought they were just sparks. Naturally he said that ones in New Orleans were much larger.[37]

When considering the spiritual side of General Fields, it soon becomes evident that he was not all pomp and dignity. In February 1885, Fields was spending his nights at the Merchants Hotel. One evening during a cold snap, a number of icicles broke off the eaves and came crashing down through a skylight, breaking several panes of glass in the process. While the event did create an air of consternation among the other guests, the effect it had on Fields was totally unexpected. Aroused from his slumber by the crash of breaking glass,

Fields declared that ghosts were promenading on the roof and he quickly dove into the office closet to hide. Hotel managers were able to dislodge him from his safe haven only after much pleading and several threats. [38]

The summer of 1885 was a real scorcher, and one-time rumors were circulating about the camp that Fields was opening up a lemonade stand. The truth of the matter was that Fields actually *terminated* a lemonade stand, at least for the day. The actual story unfolds like this: A group of street urchins, about a dozen or so, established a lemonade stand in front of the *Times* office. They had manufactured a fair amount of the thirst-quenching liquid, which appeared to be of high quality. For some reason, during the day business had been somewhat lacking. Then towards evening along came General Fields. He sampled the elixir and made a deal with the boys to treat everyone in the crowd for the grand sum of thirty cents. The dealers were overjoyed! Then the money changed hands, and Fields signaled up the street. Out of nowhere, approximately a score of youngsters bore down on the stand, on the run. In a flash, the lemonade jar was emptied and the invaders even started eating the lemon rind! The stand's proprietors immediately suspended business, captured their belongings, and retired to attempt to balance their books.[39]

As rumors go, the one concerning Fields' attempt to learn bullwhacking was more vastly blown out of proportion than the lemonade stand myth. He never actually tried to learn anything of the sort, but he did occasionally have a few drinks with the drivers. On one such occasion in mid-July 1885, Fields had pretty much tried to drink all the whiskey in town when he noticed a bull train stalled on Main Street in front of the saloon where he had been imbibing. Walking out front, he noticed his friend, Charley Tucker, a bullwhacker who worked for the Evans Transportation Company. Fields thought it might be some fun to fool Tucker for a while (the latter also being in his cups), and he did. Then Fields decided to chase Tucker for a while. When Fields caught up with the drunken driver, he stole the man's bullwhip—the tool and proud insignia of his trade. Now, this is where it gets tricky. Whip in hand, Fields decided to move the train on down the line, as a public service, to clear the congestion on Main Street. The pivotal problem with this maneuver was that Fields had never worked a bull rig in his life. Crack went the whip and, when he got the

Ox teams line up on a cold day in downtown Deadwood.

animals' attention, they turned around on him in their yokes. This successfully jammed and blocked both sides of Main Street. Realizing the grave nature of the situation, the General prudently retreated down a dark street and lit out for parts unknown. Officer Daffy arrived on the scene and viewed a very drunk bullwhacker, Tucker, in dire straits with his rig. Daffy recruited a few of the observing, standing drunks and, correcting the oxen and the yoke, drove the train out of the lane and saved the day.

He promptly arrested Tucker for creating a public nuisance and carted him off to jail. Most of the sober folks (bartenders) agreed that it was Fields who created the nuisance. The long arm of the law reached out and snatched up the General and off to the hoosegow he went.[40]

Soon Master Evans came to the jail and, with the help of every witness who had been on the street at the time, procured the release of his driver, Tucker. As for the General, he had to wait for a while in the cooler. At the end of three days, Fields was taken before the local magistrate and fined $1 plus court costs.

Never a quitter, Fields, in that same month of July 1885, submitted a petition to be named a delegate to the Constitutional Convention, a preface to statehood. While many of the delegates received in excess of six hundred supporters, Fields brought up the rear with a grand total of seventeen.[41]

It does not appear that Fields had a lot of spare time, but in addition to entertaining the masses, he did pursue, on occasion, normal employment. Regretfully, this was not as faithfully reported as many of his other activities. In fact, it was usually only reported when he did not succeed. One example is the brief note in October 1885 generated by the *Times* after Al Raymond hired Fields to search about the countryside for his stray horses. It took Fields four days to make the rounds among Deadwood, Rapid City, and Custer, and the *Times* seemed more than happy to report his failure when Fields returned empty-handed.[42]

As time moved on, so did General Fields, and he was last noted in Deadwood news as working as a bellhop in a Rapid City hotel in 1886, when he had a minor brush with authorities over what they considered to be a "bogus" raffle. After that he decided to go back "home" to Omaha.

Fields probably arrived in the Omaha area in the fall of 1886, but he did not have a publicized brush with Omaha's legal system until the fall of 1892. Fields had been working at various odd jobs in saloons around town when he discovered a roll of bills lying on the floor of his current saloon. The money, $40, had been dropped by a fourteen-year-old lad named Bird Weelmer. The young boy had worked on a farm for the past year, saving his money so that he could attend an Omaha business college. The major problem here was that Weelmer saw Fields pick up the roll and ran after him. Catching Fields, he held him until a police officer arrived.[43]

The very next year Fields was suspected of running a "low resort." The Omaha police arrested him for attempting to solicit women to work at his resort. Fields would have been forty-four years old when this happened, but was described in the newspaper article as "Old." Apparently his life on the frontier had not been very kind to his appearance.[44]

A few years later, the tables had turned and, in the spring of 1896, Fields was the proprietor of his own Omaha saloon. He pressed charges against a vagrant named Fred Brown who was also known on the streets as "Muggins." Fields had left town for a day or so, and Muggins had stopped by the saloon and procured the keys to Fields' home. Effecting his entrance to the residence, Muggins prepared himself a fine meal and then pilfered a number of household items. Fields, "The Colored Orator of Omaha," took exception to Muggins' liberties and had him captured.[45]

A few months later, a man named Goodman was arrested for breaking and entering, and for stealing Fields' clothing. The prosecution could not prove the breaking and entering part of the accusation, but the jury did convict the man of stealing $10 worth of Fields' clothing and remanded Goodman to jail to await sentencing. While today $10 may not seem like a princely sum, in 1896 it represented a goodly amount, and the very fact that Fields had clothing worth stealing makes something of a statement about his economic position just then. The courts appeared to feel that a theft of this magnitude was a charge to be reckoned with.[46]

Just as had happened in Deadwood, Fields was often hauled in front of an Omaha judge on unprovable grounds. Such was the case that occurred around Christmas of 1897, when he was brought before Omaha's Judge Gordon. The complaint was by a fellow named Faux, who stated that he had left a trunk in the care of Fields at his residence. Faux insisted that the trunk had been opened and relieved of a bolt of cloth and other items. All the items were recovered by the police, identified by the petitioner, and returned. Thus the judge, finding no evidence of a crime, dismissed the charges against Fields.[47]

On the afternoon of June 30, 1903, Fields returned home from work and decided to tidy up his home. Taking a rug out on his second floor balcony, he leaned against the rail and began shaking the rug. The railing broke. Fields fell approximately twenty feet, breaking his neck, and is thought to have died instantly. No foul play was suspected. One Omaha paper noted that he was one of the most well known "colored" men in the city.[48] Though General Fields had departed Deadwood more than sixteen years prior to his death, his obituary was run in Deadwood's *Pioneer-Times* newspaper. Along with Calamity Jane and Wild Bill, General Samuel Fields had become a Deadwood institution, an instrumental participant in the sculpting the town's history.

CHAPTER TWELVE

CYNTHIA E. CLEVELAND: AN ACTIVIST IN THE DAKOTAS

The horror! The embarrassment! Not only had the WCTU's national vice president successfully defended a madam in court, but also it was for selling—of all things!—Demon Rum without a license. What to do about Cynthia Cleveland now?

So very often the mental image we have of women on the western frontier is that of a physically strained, often emotionally drained, haggard soul following her husband's covered wagon to a new land. Giving birth to countless unsung farm hands who have been created to assist in reaping the promised amber waves of grain. The following history sheds light on another brand of female pioneer—the women who dared stand alone in a male-dominated work force. And while capable of doing a hard day's work, getting sweaty and dirty, she was also a master of complex thoughts and original ideas.

Like the vast majority of folks who gathered in the Black Hills after

Custer verified the presence of gold, Cynthia Eloise Cleveland came from elsewhere and was headed somewhere else in the future, but before it all ended she would have a most dramatic effect on the Dakotas.

Born in Canton, New York, in 1845 to a family with a solid American Revolutionary War background,[1] Cynthia was educated at local schools and the Medina Free Academy.[2] Because Cynthia's mother was frail, and Cynthia was the oldest child, the latter handled all the hard work around the house. The girl had a phenomenal memory and a love of books and learning, but the rigors of caring for the house and being a full-time student began to erode her health and she was forced to quit school the year before she was to graduate.[3]

In 1875, when Cynthia was thirty years old, her family moved to Pontiac, Michigan, where she lived at 173 Saginaw Street and made a living by selling "fancy goods."[4] A short time later her family moved again, this time to Nebraska. Not wanting to lose her job, Cynthia stayed in Michigan. For the first time she discovered an unusual commodity: spare time.

Cynthia came into contact with a group of like-minded women in the Women's Christian Temperance Union (WCTU), and through that organization became certified as an "evangelist" for these anti-alcohol crusaders. The fact that she appeared in the public record on the 1880 National Census with her occupation was listed as "lecturer" gives ample proof of the major effect the WCTU had on Cynthia.[5] After a four-year association with the organization, Cynthia was offered an appointment by the national office as president of the Women's Christian Temperance Union in the Dakotas. While that may sound impressive, we should bear in mind that she was also the sole member of the WCTU in the Dakotas.

Cynthia Cleveland had moved there in 1880. Crossing into Nebraska to visit her family en route, she encountered her first obstacle, a blizzard. The worst snowstorm of the winter of 1879–1880 greeted her, but on she went. In her own words, as part of a report to the WCTU's national office, her beginnings in Dakota Territory went like this:

> *After Miss Willard appointed me organizer of Dakota [Territory], I left my Michigan home in January of 1880, for my field of labor. I was blockaded seven weeks by snow in a frontier town in*

Cynthia Cleveland's gentle countenance belied her tenacity.

Nebraska, where my family lived. Four weeks of the seven the settlement was without flour, having to grind their corn and wheat as well as they could in a large coffee mill, owned by one of the settlers for grinding [cattle] feed. . . . From the [post-blizzard] flooded section I went to central and northern Dakota, laboring in the Black Hills, at the military posts and in the railroad and river towns. The work has been mostly missionary in its character, but we trust the foundation is laid for effective organization another year. The press has treated me kindly, and the people have welcomed me with true frontier hospitality.[6]

What Cynthia did not mention were the negative aspects of local concern that she would encounter in the Dakotas, especially in the Black Hills. Temperance representatives had been delivering their messages in the Hills since 1877, with the first known being Captain W. A. Beard representing the Reform Temperance Club in May of that year.[7]

The captain had come from New Bedford, Massachusetts, to open a grocery store in Deadwood. In addition to his aversion to liquor, he was a strong advocate of the railroad's coming to Deadwood. Many people at the time thought these ideas to be at opposite ends of the economic spectrum, with many in Deadwood fearing that an end to the liquor traffic in Deadwood would severely weaken the economic stability of the town as a whole. In 1878, the *Black Hills Daily Times* published an article that claimed that the temperance movement was "like a tidal wave moving westward from Yankton [Dakota Territory]."[8]

Also in 1877, Murphy's Blue Ribbon movement had made it to Deadwood, and then there was a Red Ribbon Club in 1879, holding meetings and attempting to raise the ire of the average citizen against the evils of alcohol. All of these strong national organizations perhaps worried the average citizen only rarely, but absolutely horrified those who lived for strong drink, or made their living from it.[9]

Naturally, the folks advocating temperance came under the most intense scrutiny by local observers, and on May 17, 1878, when a number of temperance workers were said to be seen in a public drinking establishment, it made the news, and—true or false—some damage was done.[10]

Local residents considered many of the temperance folks to be akin to carpetbaggers, out to win influence, gain power amid the maelstrom of frontier life, and somehow make money. In March 1881, the editor of the *Black Hills Daily Times* ran an editorial stating that he felt that "Prohibition would have a greater economic impact on Deadwood than the Great Deadwood fire [of 1879] had."[11]

Cynthia Cleveland arrived in the Black Hills in July 1881. Entering Deadwood, she presented herself at the offices of the *Black Hills Daily Times*. When she left that place of business, she took with her nothing less than their respect and praise. They ran the following statement after her visit:

> *This Lady honored our office with a visit. We were impressed with her earnestness and lady-like deportment. In the great cause for which she is working we wish her abundant success. This week she lectures and works in Lead, the next in Central, and the week following here. She comes with the highest recommendations. She is endeavoring to engage the Gem Theater for her work. We bespeak for her earnest attention and respectful treatment.*[12]

By July 12, having lectured only in Lead, Cynthia had convinced more than one hundred Leadites to sign her Temperance Pledge.[13] From Lead, Cynthia went to Central City. Her strategy was as simple as it was compelling. The first half-hour of lecture was for the children, and then she turned her attention to the "grown male sinners."[14]

She lectured at Central City until July 22 and then went to Terraville. At Terraville she used the school and invited everyone. As she had done previously in Central City, Cynthia spoke first to the children and then to the adults.[15] Known as Clara to those who followed her, Cynthia Cleveland worked hard: after giving an evening lecture in Terraville, she would rise early, walk down the mountain-side to Central City to attend services at St. Paul's Methodist Church, and then give a temperance lecture in the early afternoon.[16]

Cynthia made her way to Deadwood at the end of July. She started her lecture series at the Lawrence County courthouse on Sherman Street. The First Methodist Episcopalian congregation used the courthouse as their church at this early date, and Cynthia was going to be in the pulpit that morning and then again that evening.[17] The next day she rented Nye's opera house. As before, she maintained her established and successful formula. The *Times* reported, "The order of proceedings this evening will be as follows: Children's meeting at 7 o'clock, workers' meeting at 7:30 and the regular proceedings at 8 o'clock. A general invitation is extended to everybody. Admission is free."[18]

On the same day as her scheduled lecture at Nye's, Cynthia was observed making the rounds to all of Deadwood's saloons, decorating the counters with handbills inviting the clientele to come and hear her "gospel lecture" on temperance that evening. The *Times* reporter, always having the last word, stated at the end of the article, "We presume, as it is dull times, they will all go and take the pledge."[19]

It turned out that the reporter was correct, and fifty-five of Deadwood's young men and women took the pledge. Cynthia informed the *Times* that she was still somewhat uneasy with the turnout, because she had not seen any of Deadwood's businessmen at her lectures. So, the *Times*, always obliging, went on to say, "She wants the old sinners to come out, and [see] if she can't do them good before they are lost beyond redemption."

In addition to Cynthia's temperance lectures, she also gave a lecture for the ladies on the "Progress of Temperance Reform and the Outlook of the Work."[20] In the short span of three days, Cynthia had swayed the Deadwood press into believing that her cause was just and her was approach logical, and her views anything but fanatical. The *Times* noted that

> *Miss Cleveland, one of the most worthy ladies engaged in the temperance work, and an eloquent lecturer, will speak this evening, or rather resume her course of lectures at Nye's opera house. The lady is a conscientious worker, strong in her convictions and has the faculty of presenting her view on the subject in a manner calculated to inspire confidence. She does not insult her audiences by indiscriminate denouncement and reckless charges. Go and hear her.*[21]

In the same issue, Cynthia published her "Sure Cure for Drunkenness." She related the story of a well-known English sea captain, Vine Hall, commander of the *Great Eastern* steamship. The man had taken to constant drinking and long periods of drunkenness. When he decided that he had enough of it, "his utmost efforts to regain himself proved unavailing." Captain Hall sought the advice of an eminent physician who gave him the following prescription:

> *Phosphate of Iron, five grains*
> *Magnesia, ten grains*
> *Peppermint water, eleven grains*
> *Spirit of Nutmeg, one drachma. . . .*

Cynthia declared that the prescription acted as a tonic and a stimulant, and would cure the physical and moral decline that often accompanies sudden cessation of "stimulating drinks."[22] Regretfully, none of the local papers ran any tributes to the success of her cure.

In the early days of July, reporters had commented that Cynthia Cleveland drew crowds because times were slow. By the end of July, pay dirt was hit overlooking Spearfish Canyon and the new camp of Carbonate exploded onto the scene. As if pulled by a vacuum, all the unemployed miners and all the speculators vanished from Deadwood. The new "Carbonate Camp" occupied much of the news.[23] When the second Carbonate Mining Company opened—with shareholders such as the Adams Brothers, Jake Shoudy, Sol Star, and Seth Bullock—it seemed obvious to everyone that Carbonate was the up-and-coming place of concern.

Because of the Carbonate "rush," Cynthia's lectures had not been attracting the large audiences she desired, so she changed her lecture schedule from twice a day to every other night. In the opening days of August 1881, Cynthia was often able to have two articles concerning her work published in a single issue of the *Black Hills Daily Times*. This was no small feat. The *Times* noted that she was probably "the best single handed talker who ever visited the Hills." The article then went on to indicate that "it would do the old sinners of Deadwood a world of good to go and hear her at least once."[24]

Cynthia succeeded in making a "tough sell" idea eminently palatable, if not downright delectable, in a town where "sin" was the Main Street mainstay. Part of her success was the variety of subjects that she lectured on. Her subjects varied from "The Domestic to the Political," and from "Our Young Folks" to "Liquor Traffic and Taxation." Her abilities and variety led one *Times* reporter to say "Miss Cleveland's lectures are all fresh, interesting and instructive—a genuine intellectual treat to even those who delight in looking upon the wine when it is red."[25] Cynthia was making such a profound impression on the entire city of Deadwood and its satellite camps that the *Times* was compelled to write a long article on her work. It summed up Cynthia's approach in this way: "A prominent trait of Miss Cleveland's character is her good, sound, solid sense, unwarped by prejudice or fanaticism, and for that reason she can command a respectful hearing and even a hearty welcome from drinking and saloon men, when a rabid partisan would be shown the door."[26]

Cynthia had convinced 455 of the local population to take her temperance pledge. The demographics looked like this: Deadwood—116, Lead—114, Central City—69, Terraville—34 (with the work there not yet complete), Custer—46, Rockerville—35, Rapid—20, Spearfish—19, with Crook City, Sturgis, and Fort Meade not yet canvassed. She also succeeded in organizing the Deadwood Chapter of the Women's Christian Temperance Union, with Mrs. Charleton as president and Mrs. Pelton and Mrs. Jones as vice presidents.[27] In other areas of Dakota Territory, Cynthia's progress and the fact that she succeeded in forming a temperance union in that rowdiest of environments, Deadwood, did not go unnoticed.[28]

With a large percentage of the male population having vanished from Deadwood by August 11, 1881, Cynthia decided that she needed to see what all the excitement was about. She borrowed a horse and visited the Carbonate Camp on horseback. She was in "ecstasy," having never been witness to the sudden and abrupt changes that gold could have on a population, and amazed at the rush, hurry, and enterprise of the people.[29]

A week later, after having delivered lectures to every mining camp she could find in the Black Hills, Cynthia climbed aboard the Sidney Stage for a short run to Rapid City. During her four-week stay in the Hills she had garnered five hundred signatures to the temperance pledge. After visiting Rapid City, she intended a short stay in Pierre and then would push on to tour the northern portion of the territory.[30]

In early September 1881, Cynthia arrived in Bismarck and began a series of lectures at the Methodist Episcopal Church. She opened the evening with a lecture on "The Progress of Temperance Reform and the Outlook for the Future."[31] Her absence did not dissuade the Deadwood papers from following and publishing her progress, thus on September 6 the *Times* editor recommended that his contemporary at the *Bismarck Tribune*, "Brother [Clement A.] Lounsberry," should perhaps seek out Cynthia's medicine, "administered without money and without price."[32] The *Bismarck Tribune* announced her arrival with this short but telling article:

> *Miss Cynthia Eloise Cleveland, of the National Temperance Union, is in the city to aid in organizing a temperance work. She is vice president of the Women's Temperance Union, of Sixth Congressional District of Michigan, and is a lecturer of some note. She held her first meeting at the Methodist Church last evening, and will speak again on Friday evening, The Detroit and other Michigan papers speak in high terms of Miss Cleveland as a lecturer and as a highly cultivated lady.*[33]

That fall, Cynthia was ready to report the progress of her labors to her peers at the national meeting of the WCTU in Washington, D.C. At its meetings, Cynthia declared that she would become a resident of the Dakotas.[34] As the conference went on, the *Times* stated that the WCTU was proud to have "Miss Clara E. Cleveland" representing the brains and beauty of Dakota Territory.[35] A Bismarck paper recounted:

> *Miss Cynthia Cleveland, of Dakota, told the story of her work in that territory, its trials and dangers, and its grand results. She had gone into the saloons in the Black Hills and urged the rugged but warm-hearted miners to take the pledge. She had never been insulted; no woman could be insulted in that country, for the sex was held in perfect reverence. It is a fascinating field of work and one in which a woman's influence could accomplish almost anything.*[36]

At the end of November 1881, Cynthia returned to the Dakotas from the WCTU national meeting. She had been elected vice president of the entire Women's Christian Temperance Union, and was beginning a series of lectures in Yankton.[37] While there, Cynthia again caught the attention of the Black Hills press when the *Times* reported her assertion that "[I]t was believed by hundreds of people that President Garfield was murdered by whiskey—that his physicians insisted upon giving him alcoholic stimulants in the face of protests of the temperance element, and that in the end he died—not from the bullet of the assassin, but a victim of whiskey." Garfield had been shot by an assassin on July 2, 1881, and lingered until September 19. The bullet that entered his back could not be located. Because doctors didn't yet understand the need for sterile conditions, an infection ensued, which caused a fatal heart attack. With apologies to Cynthia, strong spirits applied to physicians' hands and instruments might have saved the young president.

Needless to say, such comments could not go unnoticed, and the *Times* noted: "This is a new revelation in the [assassination] case which should at once be communicated to the innocent prisoner at the bar. It might save his precious neck."[38] Cynthia had never been considered fanatical by the local press, but her presidential comment did raise more than a few eyebrows in the Black Hills. At the end of December, when the *Times* got wind of her whereabouts, they published this short but telling paragraph: "Miss Cleveland, the temperance lecturer, passed through Huron on Saturday last for Pierre where she now is. If possible let her come back and visit Deadwood, as she would meet with a hearty reception."[39]

Soon after that, the *Chamberlain Register* announced in January of 1882 that "Miss Cleveland has bought a lot here and is having a building put up. This will henceforth be the headquarters of the Christian Women's Temperance Union in the Dakotas. All letters to Miss Cleveland should be directed to Chamberlain, Dakota [Territory]."[40]

In March 1882, during the worst blizzard of the season, Cynthia set out for the new town of Highmore. She located a claim of 160 acres on March 4, and began occupying the land. She maintained her claim as a squatter for six months until the property came onto the market, and then she made her final proof as a pre-emptor. When Cynthia proved up, all of her witnesses claimed that she had initially built a house on the claim and broke up five acres of land. In Cynthia's own testimony, she states that she built a home on the property, readied five acres for planting, and started corn and potatoes. In addition she also created a subsistence garden. One of Cynthia's witnesses said that she built a ten-foot by twelve-foot house with a door, windows, and a shingled roof. In addition to the house, he stated that she also built a five-foot by ten-foot stable.[41]

In the summer of that year, Cynthia was called away from her homestead to take care of temperance business, which she considered her primary objective. She issued a call for the first Dakota Territorial WCTU convention. For the WCTU of Dakota Territory, this event was the link that would give them recognition in the national organization. During the convention, they established an infrastructure, electing Cynthia as president, Carrie Kirk of Richland as corresponding secretary, and Mrs. L. I. Robinson of Sioux Falls as recording secretary. At this first convention, Cynthia summed up the products of her WCTU labors since she had arrived in 1880:

> *The work last year was almost wholly of a missionary character. During the three years, 1880, 1881, and 1882 so far, I have organized twenty-two unions, most of those having been organized since last October's national convention, at which I was made president of the territorial union, and urged to get the people to organize. I have held 216 mass meetings, and secured 3,242 signatures to the total abstinence pledge.*[42]

When all was said and done, Cynthia returned to Highmore to tend her land, and bring in her crop of corn and potatoes. On October 12, she started running her "Final Proof" notice in a Pierre newspaper, and it ran until November 16. Today her tenacity and spunk might seem unusual, but at the time, many intelligent young women were drawn to the Dakotas in a quest for land and economic independence. A Pierre newspaper ran an article about a young female schoolteacher who had come to the Dakotas from her teaching job in Illinois, three years before. The young lady had taken a farm, built a shanty on it and lived there. When writing back to her hometown newspaper she said, "I own 320 acres of land worth $2000 good money. This is the product of my own labor in three years. If any of my sister teacher[s] in the east, who toil from one year[']s labor to another—followed suit, they will be happier, richer,

RARE BARGAINS

IN

CYNTHIA E. CLEVELAND'S

ADDITION

TO

HIGHMORE, DAKOTA.

HIGHMORE.—ITS HISTORY.

In March, 1882, I took the Dakota land fever. I had been there two years traveling over the territory lecturing on temperance and organizing W. C. T. U's as President of that organization for Dakota under National appointment. I had been perfectly sure all the time that I should never get the fever, but I did, suddenly and bad. I began investing in town lots, in a temperance woman's small way (small financially I mean), making one hundred per cent. on some investments in a short time and less on others. The next thing was to get a claim. My first thought was Hand County, but a Presbyterian minister of my acquaintance who had gotten a claim at Highmore, said I was foolish to go there when I could strike a future county seat town by going to Highmore. So to Highmore I went. The great rush in Dakota is for the county seat towns. My first visit to the claim was March [illegible]th, 1882, through the worst blizzard of that winter. At that time there was but one man and the section house folks in the county. I was a squatter for more than six months, but at last the land came into market and I made my final proof as a pre-emptor. It is the only town in the county, is almost exactly the geographical center, is

ON THE MAIN LINE OF THE NORTHWESTERN RAILROAD,

nearly midway between the cities of Huron and Pierre, and is just the location for the *Chief City between these points.* It is in the midst of as fine a stock raising and agricultural section as the widely advertised counties of Hand, Sully and Hughes, which surround it. Though the first land in this county was subject to filing only last September it already has a large population of thrifty, intelligent farmers from the States. There are still good openings for every line of business at this point. But this is the *last chance* to invest in a *new County Seat Town* (which, this will be very soon), along the main line of the Northwestern Railroad. While here soliciting for the college, as announced in *The Inter Ocean* of May 25th, I shall be from two to four o'clock, P. M., each day at the office of Kimball, Vose & Co., Room 19, Tribune Building, to negotiate sales of this property.

CYNTHIA E. CLEVELAND.

An advertisement offering land in "Cleveland's Addition" near Highmore in the Dakota Territory.

wiser, and show a better chance at getting married."[43]

After Cynthia proved up on her own claim, she had it platted as the Cleveland Addition of Highmore, Dakota Territory, then subdivided the property and prepared to sell lots on the market.[44] In addition to her original 160 acres, she purchased more, bringing her total Highmore holdings to 480 acres.[45]

This began a series of socially disastrous interactions with the Dakota territorial governor. Cynthia attempted to convince Governor Nehemiah G. Ordway that it would be appropriate to make Highmore the new county seat. Her land was situated immediately west of, and connected to, the platted town of Highmore. It appears that Governor Ordway was not very interested in her plan.

Rumors had it that when Cynthia's requests to the governor failed, she then offered to split any and all profits with him.[46] Her personal letter somehow fell into the hands of Ordway's private secretary—who promptly turned it over to the press. A Pierre editor said, about the assumed author of the letter,

> *such things are to be expected from that class of "short haired" women scading [sic] through the country in quest of notoriety, claiming to be the champions of their down trodden sex, the advocates of freedom and the leaders in a much needed reform; who claim the right to occupy the pulpit and rostrums, to practice the learned professions, Stump the country, and in fact do anything but stay at home and discharge its duties, like good sensible true Christian women ought to do. It is not that the world cares what professions the Anthonies [Susan B. Anthony and other suffragists], the Clevelands [temperance workers] and all the other such cranks practice if they attend to that business like other business people do, but they make themselves ob[v]ious in the agitation of imaginary evils, for the sole purpose of notoriety.*[47]

Soon after Cynthia had finished the business of establishing her homestead, she departed for Pierre, where she petitioned Alonzo Jay Edgerton, chief justice of the Dakota Territory Supreme Court, for her admittance to the territorial bar. On Wednesday, October 18, 1882, she was accepted, and Cynthia Cleveland became the first female lawyer in the territory.[48] It would appear the six months of homesteading had been spent studying for the bar exam, although in her political novel, *See-Saw*, she speaks of having read many law books out loud to one of her brothers because he had vision problems.[49]

Several months later, Judge Edgerton appointed her as the public defender for a relatively high-profile case. Ironically, the case against Adah Williams, a madam, was for selling liquor without a license. Perhaps this case was designed to test Cynthia's mettle, but regardless of the obvious undercurrents of a staunch temperance worker (of no small standing) defending a liquor peddler, she won the case. The echo of her legal prowess was heard even back in the mining camps.[50] Though the victory may have gained her friends in the Dakota hinterlands, it brought criticism from temperance groups in Pierre and the East, when WCTU leaders began to question her dedication and devotion to the temperance cause. The attacks on Cynthia's moral fiber and character were noticed and commented on by news organs throughout the Territory, such as in this brief article from Bismarck:

> *Miss Cleveland, who talked temperance in Bismarck and other portions of Dakota, is now practicing law in Pierre. She was recently assigned to defend the keeper of a bawdy house—a woman—for the illicit sale of intoxicating liqueurs, and did her work so well that her client was acquitted. Now some of the awful, awful good people of Pierre censure Miss Cleveland for having done her duty. Singular that the heart of a woman goes out in sympathy for all persons in distress except the unfortunate ones of her own sex. The man who boasts of the families he has ruined, or lives in one almost constant debauch is treated kindly and received in almost any society, but the woman who makes one false step is gone forever, so far as the entreat of her own sex is concerned. Even those disposed to treat her kindly are criticized as Miss Cleveland is now criticized.*[51]

In a one paragraph brief, the *Dakota Register* of Chamberlain summed up the problem very well:

Grand Forks has a woman carriage painter, and she is pronounced the best in the place. Pierre has a woman lawyer, and she gets away with all the other lawyers and acquits her clients. The other lawyers and some of the newspapers are mad about it and are abusing her for it. Pass it around gentlemen, and abuse every criminal lawyer in the country; you have just as much right to.[52]

Cynthia now decided to concentrate on her law practice, as noted in the *Hawk Eye* of Burlington, Iowa. "Miss Cynthia Eloise Cleveland; the only lady lawyer in Dakota, and widely and well known as the president of the Dakota W. C. T. U., has concluded to enter upon the active practice of her profession."[53]

As though oblivious to local criticism over the Adah Williams case, Cynthia almost immediately set out on a new quest, making it her business to ensure that the young people of Pierre had access to higher education. To accomplish this mission, she set off on a tour of the East Coast to solicit funds from the "prosperous Presbyterians of the East."[54] Not being one to do anything halfway, Cynthia went to the top, soliciting donations from the governor of New York, her distant cousin Grover Cleveland. Cynthia apparently succeeded, lauded in the *Dakota Journal* for her "energy and enterprise." The article went on to inform the public that the Presbyterian University of Southern Dakota was incorporated on July 9, 1883, and that it would be open for students at the end of September. Freshman tuition for that term would be $13, or $40 for the entire year.[55]

Cynthia appears to have been a highly visible fixture in the Pierre scene during that year, when she boarded at Reed's Hotel on Pierre Street.[56] This may also have marked the point where Cynthia began severing her ties with the WCTU.[57] That August, the "Union Temperance" group held a meeting at the Congregational Church in Pierre. The meeting was under Cynthia's direction, but three male ministers—Thompson, Mcaffee, and Norton—assisted her.[58] In October, the *Dakota Journal* suggested that "If the prohibitionists wish to do a graceful thing, let them head their ticket with the name of Miss Cynthia Eloise Cleveland[,] our talented female barrister. It would be a sort of innovation in politics, you know, and they always take with the masses.[59]

Naturally, this brought a response from Cynthia, who was working in Huron at the time. "Dear *Journal*," she wrote. "Please do not recommend me for office on the prohibition ticket, as I am a Republican prohibitionist instead of a Prohibition Party prohibitionist. Respectfully, Cynthia E. Cleveland."

Then the *Journal* proceeded to inform Cynthia that one was as bad as the other and that it would be far better for her to "attend to the duties of a lady instead of skirmishing around the Territory making a hippodrome of herself and disgracing the Republican party."[60] With comments like that from the local press, it should be no surprise that Cynthia changed over to the Democratic party, went on the warpath, and vowed her allegiance to Grover Cleveland. On July 24, 1884, the *Dakota Journal* ran a short but precise article stating that Cynthia was at the Chicago Democratic Convention, where she was treated by several of the delegates like royalty. "She is now a confirmed Democrat."[61]

Grover Cleveland received the Democratic presidential nomination. In the fall of 1884, Cynthia began actively campaigning for him in Michigan and Indiana. This activity gave her the distinction of being the first woman in the United States to campaign for a Democratic presidential candidate.[62] While stumping for Grover, Cynthia earned at least part of her living by giving lectures on popular topics of the day. In Traverse City, Michigan, she gave several lectures from that city's Methodist Church on "Washington Notes" and "Why the Desperadoes of the Frontier Came from Christian Homes." For the first lecture she did not charge an admission, and for the second lecture she requested twenty-five cents at the door.[63]

According to her first novel, *See-Saw*, after she finished stumping for Grover in Iowa and Indiana, she returned to Pierre to resume her law practice. When she arrived in Pierre, local pressure was such that she was ready to leave the territory and start over somewhere new.[64]

Cynthia had no sooner left the territory for the nation's capital than rumors began circulating that her purpose for leaving was to convince President Cleveland to appoint her as the next Dakota territorial governor as soon as Governor Gilbert A. Pierce was "decapitated."[65]

When Grover won the presidency, Cynthia began canvassing the new chief executive for a job appointment, which she felt she had earned for her work in his campaign. But the president—enemy of patronage appointments and proponent of civil service exams—steadfastly refused to acknowledge her requests.[66] So she chose to overcome the problem as she had always done in the past: study everything available on the subject. If the president would not help her, then she would help herself. She took the civil service law examination and became the first female lawyer assigned a job in the Treasury Department through the exam. Her base pay was $1,000 a year, and in early 1886 she was given a raise to $1,200 per annum.[67]

In 1887, Cynthia produced her first novel, named *See-Saw,* and it evoked a number of responses across America. In Deadwood, comments first appeared on the front page of the *Times* in November of that year. A brief article indicated that the book was creating "a stir in political and social circles, east." Then the article reminisced about Cynthia's history in the Dakotas.[68]

Five days later, another article appeared with significantly more detail on why the *Times* thought the book was so controversial. The article began by informing the reader that Cynthia's book had created "such a furor that its publishers are credited with the design of suppressing it because of promised libel suits from several of the characters, whom the author has covered but too thinly with the web of romance." Again, this article briefly recapped Cynthia's book, and stated that they thought she had entered into government service through her campaign efforts for the president, and ended by referencing her position in the government service: "From this standpoint she has written her book, and in it she has made the characters so violently personal that they recognize themselves at a glance."[69]

If the *Black Hills Daily Times* was gently negative to an old friend, the *Mitchell Daily Republican* was rabid in its attack on her work and her private life. Beginning with an immediate disclaimer that blamed the article on "Mack" of the *Sioux City Journal,* the *Republican* began an almost positive account of her life in the Dakotas. They intimated that perhaps Cynthia's very presence in the Dakotas was the result of a battlefield tragedy, when a young lieutenant in a Michigan regiment died fighting in the South in the 1860s. The paper stated that: "She clothed his memory with such heroic sacredness that she resolved never to marry." Thus ended anything positive that the article may have had to say about Cynthia.

The *Daily Republican* began its tirade by stating that, whatever the reason, Cynthia had landed in the Dakotas an old maid. As to her intelligence, the paper stated that "she had brains, even though she had a full cargo of eccentricity." They also described her appearance: "In form she was inclined to portliness, and while not a woman of beauty, there was that in her face which attracted and interested." And that "The streaks of gray that nearly whiten the once luxuriant black hair tell the story of advancing years."

From that point the article picked up a misogynistic rhythm, commenting on her failed business affairs with Governor Ordway concerning her property near Highmore, and a failed love affair with a Col. S. M. Laird. All of which, if they had happened to a man, would have been chalked up as life experiences, but since Cynthia was a woman, the items were tossed out onto the public playground.

And what of Cynthia's book? The *Mitchell Republican* dedicated twenty-seven column lines of its article to her novel, while a hundred and thirty-five lines examined the minutiae of her relationships, business deals, suspected romances, and physical attributes or lack thereof—in other words, gossip. The gist of their review is that the book is autobiographical, and that because the thin veneer of fiction had not covered the identities of the Victorian soap opera cast, the publishers resorted to pulling the books off of store shelves in order to avoid numerous libel suits.[70]

In Atchison, Kansas, the feeling toward the lady and her book was exactly the opposite of that expressed in Mitchell. The editors chose to place a line drawing of Cynthia in the article, and ventured to refute the description that Mitchell had put forth, saying:

> *She is, on the contrary, very fine looking. She is a little over middle height, has a well-rounded form and a remarkably intellectual face. Her complexion is fair, her forehead broad and intellectual, and her eyes are bright and beautiful. She talks well and her mouth is by no means an unpleasant one. Above her forehead she combs a mass of curly gray hair, which was once golden but is now mixed with silver. She dresses well and has had a most remarkable career.*

As to Cynthia's literary work, the *Atchison Globe* went on to say that *See-Saw* was not Cynthia's first work, and indicated that part of her amazing career had been spent as a journalist. *See-Saw* "is a fat volume of 200 pages, printed on heavy paper and is an actual life in the form of a novel," the Globe reported. "It is to give the voting, taxpaying masses a true representation of the life of their representatives in the departments and in congress. Miss Cleveland depicts this phase of Washington life with a master hand."[71]

Initially, Cynthia did not even put her own name to *See-Saw*, but rather the pen name "One of 'M." She obviously later recanted, because the copy that I own is inscribed "Compliments of the author, Cynthia E. Cleveland." In the preface she states, "Whether this shall prove true, we leave it to the readers to decide, for, as near as can be, it is the actual history of a life, the characters being real living facts, and only changed in name."

In my reading of the novel, it matches the known facts of Cynthia's life to a T. It also describes a woman of vision and vast political knowledge. Her persona, represented by *See-Saw*'s main character, Margaret Wayland, produces an indictment of the Republican Party of that era, addressing everything from patent monopolies on farm machinery to the centralization of wealth, stating that "Verily, the country has become a government of monopolies, by monopolies, for monopolies."[72] She makes no bones about telling the world of the evils of the Railroad Land Grant System.[73]

The *Mitchell Daily Republican* seems to have missed its mark in naming Col. Laird as the man who had jilted our Ms. Cleveland, for a later article on "The Governors' Dolls" leads the reader to a different man entirely. That article included fine line-drawings of the representative dolls submitted by the various state and territorial governors. When it came to Alaska, the article stated that Alaska governor "[Alfred P.] Swineford, notwithstanding the crosses in love which he sustained through Miss Cleveland's novel of 'See-Saw,' has sent a little Alaskan baby, which is dressed as though the thermometer was at zero, and which is brilliant in crimson cashmere. Swineford's doll is blond, and, indeed, these various governors all seem to like blond girls."[74]

In another short piece by the *Daily Republican*, they noted that "Gov. Swineford, of Alaska has made his annual report to the government, but it has no reference to the blighted affections of Miss Cynthia Cleveland."[75]

After writing her first novel, Cynthia joined forces with one of her Dakota friends, Mrs. Linda Slaughter, Bismarck's former postmistress, in 1888 to form "The Women's Press Association" in Washington, D.C., an activity that again drew the usual giggles and snorts from the boys' room.

> *Mrs. Slaughter especially has the invaluable characteristic commonly denominated as "hustle," and Miss Cynthia Cleveland has the Arizona quality of "rustle." The other ladies who have joined the band are commingled rustlers and hustlers, and they will make music for their brother pencil drivers. Unfortunately the press galleries of the house and senate are not open to these ambitious and able society letter writers. In those galleries are to be found only those who have noses for news.*[76]

Following *See-Saw*, Cynthia wrote another novel, *His Honor or, Fate's Mysteries*, which is about love on the frontier. As might be expected, in February of 1890, the *Mitchell Daily Republican* gave *His Honor* a scathing review that ended by saying "Where 'His Honor' comes in or what 'Fate's Mysteries' are does not appear, as there is no diagram attached to the book."[77] In Atlanta, Georgia, the book was noted in a slightly different light: "'His Honor,' the new Philosophical Novel, by Cynthia E. Cleveland, has already achieved an assured success."[78]

In 1890, the Washington, D.C., City Directory listed Cynthia as the sixth auditor in the Treasury Department. Her location was noted as 807 12th NW, which is five blocks from the White House lawn. It is not known as to whether this was her place of work, her home, or a boarding house.[79]

The *Mitchell Daily Republican* appears to have always wanted the last word, and thus they noted that in March 1890 that "Miss Cynthia E. Cleveland gave a reception recently to the Dakota people in Washington. Ex-Gov. Ordway, it may be said, was conspicuous by his absence."[80] She was next mentioned in the *Bismarck Tribune* in 1892 as attending "A Brilliant Reception: Mrs. Senator Hansbrough Entertains the Elite of the Capital."[81]

Following this brief and final recognition in Bismarck, Cynthia was relegated to appearing in short articles, scattered across the nation, concerning organizations that she belonged to. In 1895, the *Stevens Point*

Gazette in Wisconsin noted that the Women's National Press Association met in Atlanta, Georgia, where various ladies, including Cynthia E. Cleveland, read papers.[82] In the *Atlanta Constitution*, it was noted that the Women's Press Association had come from Washington, D.C., under the leadership of Mrs. Belva Lockwood, and the association was staying in Atlanta for a two-day conference. Cynthia gave a paper titled "Press Women and Civil Service Reform."[83] This is the earliest reference to Cynthia and Belva Lockwood associating with each other, but not the last. Mrs. Lockwood was the first woman to be admitted to the Supreme Court Bar and was also the first woman to be nominated for the presidency of the United States.

In April 1906, Cynthia and Belva Lockwood were again together as officers in the Federation of Women's Clubs. Belva reported on civil service, and Cynthia reported on a work plan that the committee had devised to better the city of Washington, D.C. Cynthia stated that the organization would push for more sanitary conditions, training of good citizens, material municipal cleanliness, and "the City Beautiful."[84] Cynthia was also a long-time member of the Women's National Press Association, and held its office of auditor during 1916 and 1917.[85] Throughout all of this, Cynthia still maintained a close relationship with her religious roots: In 1911, she held a lawn party at her home to benefit the new Union Church. Among others, the mayor of Washington and his wife attended.[86]

Cynthia graduated in 1899 from Howard University with a Bachelor of Law, and in 1900 with a Master's of Law degree.[87] At age fifty-five, Cynthia had attained her first advanced degrees.

Cynthia worked at the U.S. Treasury as auditor of the Post Office from 1886 to 1911. When she began employment with the Treasury, her annual salary had been $1,000, and it topped out at $1,400 before her retirement.[88]

In about 1902, Cynthia left her Washington home to live with her brother in Kensington, Maryland. She remained at that residence until her death in May 1932. Her obituary indicates that she was a member of the District of Columbia Bar and the Democratic Law Enforcement League. She was a life member of the Daughters of the American Revolution, and a past vice president and charter member of the League of American Pen Women.[89]

There is no way of ever knowing what Cynthia's vision for the Dakotas might have been. She was instrumental in getting constitutional prohibition into the organic laws when South Dakota became a state. Whether she ever came back to the Dakotas after becoming a social outcast in Pierre is a question that has yet be answered. The one obvious thing that she seemed to want more than anything else, love, seemed to elude her to the very end.

THE FLORMANNS: IN THE GRIP OF GOLD FEVER

Colorado, Montana, Wyoming, New Mexico, and finally the Black Hills. Then Hillyo, Deadwood, Bear Butte/Galena district, Virginia City, Rapid Creek, Boxelder Creek, Slabtown, Greenwood/Laflin. Bob Flormann just knew he'd make his fortune in mining—until others began to wonder about his methods.

When most Black Hills historians come across the name "Flormann," one of two major regional events flashes into their minds: the Greenwood Mining Swindle or the Big Bend/Fort Meade Hydraulic Mining Scandal. Armed with the names of those two events, the inquisitive reader can investigate, for days, the purported negative impact of Robert Flormann on the Black Hills. There is, however, a positive side of a would-be empire builder who was stricken with that dangerous disease, gold fever.[1]

Robert Flormann was the elder of two brothers who immigrated to the United States from Dusseldorf, Germany, in the last half of the 19th century. Robert was born in 1835 and his brother, Charles, in 1841. While it is not known where the Flormann brothers acquired their mining expertise, it is known that they worked their way across the United States at professions other than mining. Robert worked making fine pastries for a time, while in Denver, and Charles was a saloon keeper.

The brothers were probably exposed to precious metals prospecting while in Denver. Between 1858 and 1916, Denver supported a large enclave of ethnic Germans, many of whom enjoyed saloons as the centers of their social, political and economic activities. Often, these establishments also housed other vital community functions, such as bakeries. Thus, with one brother baking and the other pouring, Denver must have been very comfortable for the Flormann boys.

In gold camps throughout the West, the Flormann name became associated with the quest for both gold and silver. Before coming to the Black Hills, Robert's ventures took him and his wife, Ernestine, to the fields in Colorado, Montana, Wyoming, and New Mexico. Small hints left behind, such as the birth records of his daughter Frances (1865) in Colorado, son Louis in Montana, and daughter Florence in New Mexico, give us a brief but accurate image of a family man dedicated to his wife and children. Charles and his wife, Frederica, had three children prior to heading to the Black Hills, two born in Colorado and one in Cheyenne, Wyoming.

Robert first entered the Black Hills from the south, coming north out of Fort Russell near Cheyenne in 1875. With a grubstake from Major Wooley, the post trader at Fort Russell, he initially prospected along French Creek for placer gold and indications of quartz. His prospecting efforts took him north, where he arrived on Spring Creek near what is now Hill City on July 14. When he arrived there, a mining camp named "Hillyo" was already active. One of the miners at the Hillyo camp during this period described Robert as "The Ruling spirit" of the camp, "a big verbose German, Flormann by name. He had a splendid four horse team and a big Bain Wagon heavily loaded."

Indications are that Robert was a friend of a former mayor of Cheyenne, Mark V. Boughton, and his business partner Berry. Boughton and Berry had a sawmill in storage in Cheyenne. In 1876, Flormann introduced the men around camp and informed the miners that, with a little encouragement, Boughton and Berry would bring their sawmill to the banks of Spring

Creek. In fact, Berry had already chosen a site for his mill along those waters and the two merchants began building it in January of that year. During the winter, when little mining could be done, Robert Flormann and three other men—Miller, Harvey, and McCullough—platted the town site and organized the mining district along Spring Creek.

Robert's stay in the Black Hills thus far had convinced him that the rush was not just a flash in the pan. He was convinced that there was money to be made, and he was going to get his share. That spring, he returned to Denver for his family. April 1876 found Robert, his wife, three children and their dog returning to the Black Hills through Red Canyon, their wagons loaded with family possessions. Robert, now a seasoned veteran of the Hills, was acting as guide for a small wagon train of mostly men coming to the Hills to prospect.

On April 24, 1876, the wagon train came upon the Metz massacre. Metz had been a successful baker who had sold his business in Custer City. He had found the Black Hills a little too rough for his family and was returning south to farm. He was accompanied by his wife, a wagon driver/guide, and a black woman who worked as the Metz family cook. As was Flormann, Metz had been traveling with everything he owned in several wagons. A frugal man, Metz had saved a large portion of the money earned while he was in Custer, and he carried that in addition to the $1,000 he made from selling his bakery. The Flormann group found the Metz party dead. They had been attacked, killed, and robbed. The contents of their wagons were strewn across the massacre site, as though an armed, deliberate search had been conducted. The prospectors, miners, and businessmen who were accompanying the Flormann train panicked and "were going make a run for Custer City, when Flormann pulled out his revolver and threatened to shoot any man who attempted to desert them." The men were afraid that "the Indians" were still lurking about, and did not want to risk another attack. In the end, the men became more afraid of Flormann than of the "Indians," and they stayed to help take the Metz bodies to town.

Ernestine Flormann prepared Mrs. Metz's body for the trip, but the family cook could not be found that day. Searchers later discovered her body some distance from the Metz family, with an arrow in her back and five dollars clutched in her hand. After they returned the black lady to town for a proper burial, that five dollars found its way to the local saloon where it purchased a round for the search party. While in Custer, Robert spread the word that he did not believe that Indians had attacked the Metz party. None of the Metz cash was found at the massacre site. Robert was of the opinion that Indians would not have searched so methodically, nor would they have taken paper money or gold.[2]

After safely reaching Deadwood, Robert examined all of the resources in the area before purchasing Placer Claim No. 11 above Discovery. The owner of Claim No. 10, George Stokes, stated that Flormann established a cabin on Claim No. 11 for his wife and children. Stokes went on to describe Mrs. Flormann as a good German wife who believed in the "three German K's—Kinder, Kuchen and Kirche, Children, Cooking and Church." He added that, while she didn't find much church in the area, she gave birth to several children and was a prize cook.[3]

Accompanying the Flormann train to the Deadwood area were former Cheyenne mayor Mark V. Boughton and his business partner Berry, with components of their sawmill. The mill was initially set up on the site of the current (and third) Lawrence County Courthouse on Sherman Street.[4] By the following April, one newspaper would report that, between James May's saw mill and that of Boughton and Berry, "there need now be no trouble about getting lumber."[5]

One of the problems in a gold rush environment was establishing a consistent value on gold. In June, newcomers Boughton and Berry were part of a coalition of thirty-five Deadwood merchants that fixed the value of gold-as-payment in Deadwood at $18 per ounce.[6]

The news of the day on September 23, 1876, was that "Bob Floorman" had discovered a 40- to 60-foot bed of clay and gravel that crossed Claim No. 11 diagonally, and was showing good color.[7] His fortunes as a gold-seeker were on the rise.

But in 1876, Flormann wasn't relaxing in his relative prosperity. In October, a paper reported that "Floorman" had shown the editor "the richest specimen of argentiferous [silver-bearing] ore we have ever seen in the Hills."[8] The vein was surrounded by "hard brownish quartzite."

In February 1877, Robert claimed the Florence Lode in the Bear Butte/

Galena district, the source of that sample. (The Bear Butte/Galena mining district would encompass today's Galena ghost town east of Lead and Bear Butte northeast of Sturgis. On modern roads, the distance between them is about 35 miles, from Galena through Lead, Deadwood, Sturgis, and Fort Meade.)

Newspaper accounts of Flormann's Galena-area site are sometimes confusing, calling the mine both the Florence Mine and the *Flormann* Mine. Flormann had named the mine after his youngest daughter. Whichever name they called Flormann's first lode, area miners sat up and took notice. For simplicity, we'll call it the "Flormann Mine" here.

Soon, Robert's workers had driven the tunnel to a depth of 80 feet. It was reported to have ten tons of ore awaiting processing that would average $2,000 a ton. (Two years later, an assay report cited by a Deadwood newspaper gave its value as $1,113 per ton, adding that "This mine bids fair to exceed in richness any of the old established mines of Nevada.")[9]

Following another vein, Flormann miners broke into underground caves—ready-cut tunneling big enough for a man to walk into.

Immediately, the town of Virginia City was platted at the junction of Spring Run and Bear Butte Creek. It was easily accessible via new roads connecting to Custer, Rapid City, Fort Pierre, and Bismarck, so that "the new settlement [would be] one of the most desirable places in the Hills." The *Times* went on to editorialize that "There is a fine field open in this district for capitalists, and we respectfully invite their attention."[10] Underground mines required investors supplying capital. In such places, miners became employees, earning paychecks instead of hoping for a personal bonanzas.

Robert was now seriously looking for "capitalists" to invest in his finds. By April, he had sold Placer Claim No. 11 in Deadwood in order to devote all of his time to his new Galena diggings. The *Black Hills Weekly Times* reported that "the new owners of No. 11 are running on Floorman's [sic] old tailings. It pays $10.00 a day to the man."[11] The writer failed to say how many men were working the tailings, the term for unprocessed rock that earlier mining had left behind.

That February, Robert sold the Flormann silver mine to "Capt. Davies," John H. Davey, for $50,000.[12] Flormann took over the nearby

:" as a host-
Vhip," who
ance for the

e opens to-
The opening
edy entitled
dand," to be
rama, "The
The simple
anager Lan-
pirit of this
amusement,
antee to our
enjoy a first
n.

ggists, Gay-
load of car-
fer the trade

double bed
nen: Terms
om without
quire at the
treet.

New Xork office, 23 Fifth Avenue.

Chicago office, 54 Clark Street.

Deadwood office, Main Street

W. L. HALL, Agent.

SALOONS.

FLORMANN'S STAR SALOON.

Just opened opposite Pacific Hotel is a Gem in every sense of the word. The Bar is supplied with the Choicest Brands of

IMPORTED LIQUORS,

WINES

AND

CIGARS.

Mr. Flormann ss a master in the mixing up of as reliable a drink as can be obtained in the Hills. Remember the

STAR SALOON

opposite Pacific Hotel, keeps the choicest imported Liquors.

C. FLORMANN, Proprietor.

OOKS AND STATIONARY.

FICE ... E

Black Hills Pioneer Oct 27, 1877

At the Star Saloon, Charles Flormann touted his abilities as a master mixologist and his stock of the "choicest imported liquours."

Rutherford B. Hayes and the Yellow Jacket No. 2, the latter boasting assays of $500 to $5,000[13]

Charles Flormann moved north from Cheyenne to join his brother in 1877 and established the Star Saloon across the street from the Pacific Hotel in Gayville—just southwest of then-Deadwood on Deadwood Creek. (That settlement was named for its founder, William Gay.) Charles described himself in a large advertisement as "a master of mixing up of as reliable a drink as can be found in the Hills."[14] Soon, though, Charles would also contract the gold fever.

But as1877's original gold rush slowed, Robert Flormann and other miners looked for new opportunities. One was hydraulic mining, which used powerful streams of water to bring down the gravel embankments containing gold or silver. Men forced this displaced gravel through sluices and recovered its precious metal. The process had proven successful in California, and some wanted to try it in the Black Hills. Articles concerning the profitability of hydraulic mining began to appear in Black Hills newspapers as early as 1877.

Of course, Deadwood miners began to rush to Galena. Two years later, as a large silver mill readied to open in the latter, a Galena resident wrote to a Deadwood paper urging miners from that area to stay away. Galena/Bear Butte area workers had been promised first chance for employment at the new mill. "Jake" cautioned: "It would be very unpretty to have a lot of new men rush in here for work after we'ns [sic] have waited patiently for three years for something to turn up...."[15]

In the spring of 1877 Robert Flormann traveled to the East looking for investors, just as Deadwood miners became interested in hydaulicking.[16] When he returned home, Robert joined the hydraulic movement.

By the spring of 1878, the Park Pool Hydraulic Company was reportedly working on Whitewood Creek near Deadwood. This company proposed bringing water in from a point two miles below Galena and combining it with the water from Twobit Creek to provide enough for the hydraulic monitor.[17]

Soon everyone wanted to be engaged in hydraulicking. In November 1879, a man named N. Durvie arrived in Deadwood with the news of his plans for a grand scale hydraulic works on Rapid Creek. He called it the

Fort Meade Gold Mining Company, and told the *Times* that he planned a 600-foot-long tunnel to bypass Rapid Creek's Big Bend, cutting off and draining two miles of the creek.[18] Rapid Creek's flow would no longer slow down and lose strength in its Big Bend.

That was the last anyone heard of Durvie, but the following summer, Sam Sturgis visited the Fort Meade Hydraulic works and reported being very satisfied with progress made by its new superintendent, Robert Flormann. Robert's stated plan at that time was to improve upon Durvie's idea by straightening even more of Rapid Creek.

Either way, the goal was to strengthen Rapid Creek's flow and then use it for cutting down mountainside gravel deposits. He expected his tunnel to be 700 feet long with a drop of more than 70 feet, to provide 2,000 miner's inches of water for the company's mining operations.[19]

Flormann's final version was only 554 feet long—146 laborious feet shorter than Durvie's plan and just as large inside—was finished in September 1880.[20]

In July 1881, almost a year to the day after Sturgis praised him to the skies while the tunnel was being built, Robert was fired. Robert had several aces up his sleeve, though, and when his work stopped, he stopped the company. He had no intention of going anywhere until he felt that an equitable settlement had been reached between him and Fort Meade Hydraulic. One must assume that this meant money. It seems that, while Robert did not own the company, he did hold all the water rights and mineral claims for that section of Rapid Creek. He also had something else going for him: public opinion. The editor of the *Black Hills Daily Times* described Robert's work for the Fort Meade Hydraulic Company as "both square and efficient," and said that under his guidance, the company's work had been "pushed foreword [*sic*] as rapidly as possible."[21]

For many folks, this probably would have marked the end of their involvement with the area, but not Robert. He appeared in Deadwood the fall of 1881 looking to secure a winter grubstake. His plan now was to gain control of as many claims below the Fort Meade works as he could and form a new company named the "Big Bend Hydraulic Mining Company." To this end, Robert successfully worked to be elected as recorder of the Ruby Mining District along Rapid Creek. He merged many placer claims

Robert Flormann built the Windsor Block in 1886 to house a grocery and department store on the street level and rented rooms above.

on the creek below the Fort Meade Company's property, eventually controlling eighty-six.

Here is where things begin to get a bit murky; it is not clear how many of the claims he owned and how many he only leased. One report states that he leased claims valued at $80,000. Having said that, there is some evidence that he may personally have owned all the claims, and then leased them to the newly formed Big Bend Hydraulic. Regardless, after Robert acquired his claims, he traveled east to secure financial support from "capitalists," or investors. Robert must have been very successful with this venture because, in April 1883, Big Bend Hydraulic was incorporated under the laws of the State of New York. That same year he published the first report to the company's shareholders.

Robert and his family now lived full time in Rapid City, while he spent his days on Rapid Creek. He also invested in the town by building a total of four brick business blocks, including the now-restored Windsor Block on St. Joseph Street.[22]

In June 1883, Robert had a close call. He was attempting to cross Rapid Creek near the Fort Meade tunnel when his team and wagon were swept away by the current. Leaping out of the wagon, Robert swam ashore and ran along the creek, following his wagon and struggling team of horses downstream. For a quarter of a mile he followed them and then they got caught up in a small eddy. The eddy slowed them down enough that Robert was able to swim out and cut the harness, saving the horses but losing the wagon.

At about this same time Robert reportedly leased Big Bend Hydraulic's property, yet the works would sit silent for the next four years. The Big Bend and Fort Meade properties may have sat inactive because Robert became distracted with new prospects. In the spring of 1884, Robert and his son, Louis, were investigating new digs on Boxelder Creek in Lawrence County near what was then called Slabtown, east of Sturgis. That June, Louis worked for the survey party that established the corners of Placer Claims 404 and 403 along Boxelder Creek. These two claims became the center of the Greenwood Mining Company and the town of Greenwood.

Robert sought investors for his newest mine-and-town project. He opened a school, saloon, and general store, and built a beautiful home for his brother Charles. Charles had left his own Gayville saloon and had been mining in Black Tail Gulch the last few years but, with the offer of a home for his family and the position of foreman of the Greenwood mill, Charles reestablished himself and his family at Greenwood.

It is not known when Robert Flormann first met the infamous "Professor" Taylor who would become a major player in Greenwood. As early as 1879, local newspapers reported that Joseph Taylor, "an eminent mining expert" representing J. S. Taylor & Sons, a reputable British firm, was seeking promising mines for the firm's clients.[23] By 1881, the *Black Hill Daily Times* reported that he represented overseas capitalists with $100 million to invest in Black Hills mines. His examinations of the Welcome Group of mines in February 1883 and the Berkshire Mine in March 1883 were thoroughly covered by all the local newspapers.

By early 1884, Professor Taylor and Robert Flormann were working together on the Greenwood project. Taylor soon journeyed east to look for investors for the Greenwood works. He returned with $100,000 from Matthew Laflin, of the Laflin and Rand Powder Company of New York, to purchase the Greenwood. Taylor had promised Laflin that he himself would invest $50,000 of his own money.

Besides mining, another topic that the "eminent" Taylor spoke about, around Deadwood, was the Christian religion. He was not afraid to let his feelings be known to the miners and their families on the curse of alcohol and the sin of working on the Sabbath. Professor Taylor did not endear himself to the workers. He demanded that each morning begin with a long prayer, refused to allow alcohol sales in the settlement of Greenwood, and would not allow the mill or the mine to run on Sundays.

The Greenwood Mining Company was incorporated under the laws of Illinois with a reported operating capital of $500,000. Inspections were made, ore was tested, and workers began building a stamp mill for crushing ore at the Greenwood site.

And a grand mill it was, boasting 150 stamps. The company purchased and brought a narrow-gauge steam locomotive to Greenwood to haul ore from mine to mill. Men also constructed a sawmill, but the building and mining were happening at such a rapid pace that the sawmill could not keep up, and contracts had to be let for additional mine timbers. With all this work going on, Greenwood suddenly became more than just another camp in the hills. In a span of just months, the Boxelder Creek floodplain was transformed as Monheim and Lorey established a general store, Smith opened a saloon, and Joe Irwin of Deadwood moved to Greenwood and opened the Vienna Bakery. Then in September, the U.S. Postal Office established a facility there. Because there was already a Greenwood in the Dakotas, the town was renamed after the mine's principal investor, Laflin. Robert Flormann became its postmaster.

The Deadwood newspapers reported the activities of Greenwood/Laflin several times a week during the year of 1884, but there was a certain paucity of information specifically concerning Robert Flormann. The Rapid City newspapers, on the other hand, stayed well occupied reporting what appeared to be the orchestration of a nation builder. It was publicly reported that Robert had received $120,000 for a forty-nine percent interest in the Greenwood Mining Company, while he maintained controlling interest. With this money he began to build a three-story office building on St. Joseph Street in Rapid City, the Flormann Block (eventually he built three more business blocks there). He claimed a homestead in Meade County near Rapid City, and took out options on land near the Flormann Block with the intention of building a grand hotel. This was also the period when Robert began to woo a railroad. With trips to Chicago and promises of right-of-way, Robert must have appeared to be a very influential man in the Black Hills to the well-funded gentlefolk to the east. Then things in Greenwood began to slip.

By late fall of 1884, the Greenwood mill was almost finished, but the air was laced with rumors. During a public open house at the mill, a Deadwood reporter took several ore samples from the main ore bunker. Later, in the confines of his office, he ground the ore and tested it. Worthless! He called a colleague into his office and showed him the test results. He performed it again with the same results, which neither man seemed willing to believe. The mill ran for only a day in late December, and then Robert ordered his brother Charles to shut off the water. Accusations shot back and forth across the telegraph lines between Taylor and Flormann, and the mill sat silent.

As Robert's star had risen in Dakota Territory, the editor of the *Pierre Press* recalled knowing him in New Mexico back in 1871. The editor said that, by then, Flormann already had "made a dozen big fortunes and 'blowed' them . . . on other mining ventures. He is one of the best prospectors and miners in the world." Of course, his source for all this information was none other than Flormann himself. Supposedly, the $50,000 from selling his Flormann silver mine was "spent . . . in two years."[24]

In 1885, Taylor and Flormann again fell out, this time over running the mill on Sundays. Taylor claimed he had orders from Laflin to continue the Sunday closings; Flormann said his orders from Laflin were to run the mill around the clock and seven days a week if he wanted to. Each man sent the *Black Hills Weekly Times* a long letter "proving" that he was right. The paper printed them and billed each man for the printing charge. Taylor never paid, claiming the paper had asked him to write his side of the story. Eventually, the *Weekly Times* dismissed the whole argument as "a private controversy between two persons in which the general public" had no stake, wondering why the men "wished the public favor upon their side."[25]

Matthew Laflin ordered the mill to start up again, and when it didn't, he filed a criminal complaint against the mill workers. In January, the sheriff in Deadwood was dispatched by sleigh with warrants for arresting the workers. So many men were arrested that two sleighs needed two trips to bring them all back to Deadwood in chains. The arrests did not occur without incident, and one worker was critically injured when he resisted.

Among those arrested were Charles Flormann and Robert's son Louis. But Robert could not be found, and neither could the company's books. It was a tumultuous time in Greenwood, with warrants being approved, the mill running and the mill stopping, arrests being made, and then charges being dropped. Through it all, one thing became very clear: the only gold in Greenwood was in Professor Taylor's teeth.

After all was sorted out, Matt Laflin had a warrant issued for Taylor's arrest. It turns out that, way back when Taylor solicited Laflin's investment, he promised to put in $50,000 of his own money if Laflin would fork over $100,000. Taylor never paid his share. In his trial, Taylor also admitted that he had no connection with the established British mining-investment firm after all.

When all the smoke cleared, Taylor went to jail for a time and the papers reported that Matt Laflin had been duped out of more than $300,000. Somehow, through all the tough times, the town of Greenwood/Laflin persisted into the 1890s.

Laflin sold his interest in the Greenwood company late in 1886 to a group of Chicago investors.[26] When Professor Taylor got out of jail, he headed to Chicago where he protested the alleged wrong that had been done to him by Laflin. A final note about Taylor appeared in the news in February 1887. Reportedly, he had been hanged in Mexico for involvement in another mining scandal. Also in 1887, Charles Flormann's wife, Frederica, took possession of the two 80-acre claims along Boxelder Creek—the original Greenwood site—making improvements and paying taxes on them. The Greenwood mill burned down in 1892. So Robert and Louis Flormann's first claims that began the scandal were back under Flormann family control.[27]

By 1896, Robert Flormann had left the Lower 48 for the Klondike rush and developed mines in both Alaska and British Columbia. Another Flormann—his elder daughter Frances, now called "Frankie"—worked with him there. She had become a mining engineer and oversaw hydraulic mining on some of her father's claims in the north country. A woman mining engineer was deemed newsworthy by several U.S. newspapers in the late 1890s.[28]

Robert Flormann died of pneumonia in Nome, Alaska, on July 4, 1900. His wife Ernestine and the family took Robert's body to Seattle for burial. In a few short years, the family had left the Black Hills far behind.

CHAPTER FOURTEEN

YOUNG JIM: A DEADWOOD WAIF

Victorian-era writers and readers doted on poignant deaths and heart-breaking tales, and here a newspaper contributor indulges him- or herself and readers in memorializing one of Deadwood's unfortunates.

The fascinating history of the beautiful village of Deadwood and the surrounding Black Hills has generated a multitude of legends, controversies, myths, and outright lies, along with documented histories. Perhaps one of the most perplexing controversies concerns gunfights and violent deaths in Deadwood. The myth is that every day on the streets of Deadwood, someone met their doom in a violent manner during the gold rush's first year.

That sure would add up to a lot of folks in very short time. Checking with other historians, I see that the number falls short of that. Bob Lee gives an estimate of seven-seven violent deaths throughout the entire Black Hills region during the first two years. Having said that, I would like to emphasize the word "estimate." Who knows how many men and women left home for the Hills during 1875-1877 and never returned? Do

Childhood in early Deadwood would not have been without its charms—or perils.

bones lie at the bottom of abandoned mineshafts—buried with a hundred tons of mill tailings on top of them? How many fell victim to foul play in the wilderness of a forgotten gulch only to have their bones scattered by coyotes and rodents? Sometimes a person might die in the center of town and pass unnoticed, never to be recorded, leaving a family to wonder "Why don't he write?" Such may be the case of "The Waif of Deadwood."[1] Was the following a true story or an ill-advised spot of frontier journalism designed to entertain the mining masses?

The Waif of Deadwood

With all their roughness there is an inner womanish feeling deep down in the hearts of the men who people new frontier towns and cities. This feeling has often been demonstrated by those who bore the name of desperadoes, and the remote western states and territories can show some champion specimens, particularly in the mining districts. Protection for the young and the helpless rises in many cases to a feminine love for the object around which it centers, and the waif of Deadwood is no solitary example. Of all human beings, those untutored and coarse men delight in a manly boy, if the two qualities can be linked together, and help him build up his young fortunes with parental eagerness. Here is an exceedingly well told and pathetic little story of:

The Pride of the Family

The proprietors, and their industrious visitors also, were for a moment diverted from the contemplation of sundry piles of "chips" and some other matters pertaining to gambling, by the appearance of a small boy in their midst. He was an uncommon boy too, because no common boy would have gone of his own accord into the Minerva Saloon.

"Young chap, where did you come from, and who are you, anyhow?"

"My name's Jim, and I cum to here from Cheyenne to make stamps, like the rest of you. Don't you want a boy here, boss?"

"A boy! Good God! Major, do you hear that? The boy wants a place here. Jim's his name he says."

"Yes, and I reckon we had best take him, too; only what will we do with him, that's what I don't know. Jim, where's your folks?"

"Dun no – home I spect."

"And where's that?"

"I don't like to tell you that; and you don't know them—my folks—so what's the use in telling all about them, eh?"

"That boy is sharp, Major, sharp. And you want a place here, boy, do you?"

"Yes boss, I am looking for a place. I can shine boots and do most anything. I never cusses and swears, but I like to smoke cigar butts and whole ones, too."

"Shine, can you? Now let's see how you can shine before we hire you for steady work."

And Major Showers left the "lookout" seat at the faro game to test the capacity of the small boy who wished for a place. Major Showers was a gambler—a faro dealer; and his partner, "Doc" Puffer had earned the curses, because he had been the ruin of more than one poor fellow.

This small boy, Jim, was certainly the only small boy without an owner in Deadwood. It was a wonder how such a little waif came away there in the Black Hills. His own statement was perhaps as good as any:

"I jest kept a comin' till I got here, boss; that's the way it was."

"And that shirt of yours, Jim, ain't quite up to what we're used to here; but maybe you'll improve. You see we don't care what it costs, but we must have the best."

That was the only bargain ever made with the boy; but he became presently, and curiously too, part and parcel of the establishment. Like a rare painting or a curiosity, the lad became an attraction.

His quaint and old-mannish ways and sayings caused many a rough customer and those better bred, too, to stop and wonder at the boy.

"Whose little cuss is he, Doc?" asked Joe Bunche, a Deadwood terror, as he watched the boy till he wholly forgot and neglected his faro chips.

"Mine and the Major's."

"Young fellow, what's your name?"

"Jim."

"Jim what? Out with it quick or—"

"Jim—I don't like to tell, so I don't. My momma wouldn't like for me to tell neither. She said how I was going to be the pride of the family someday, if I was a good boy. O, I wish I could see Momma just onst. O—o!"

And a torrent of tears told the earnest love the lad had for his far-away mother. Other eyes, total strangers to such sensations, were puzzled at the effect of the boy's tears.

"Let the little chap alone, Joe! You've made him cry—and I won't have it," Doc said sharply.

"I didn't go to hurt his feelings, Doc, I only wanted to call the little one by his full name."

The desperado was actually trying to sooth and caress the lad.

"Then call him Jim Pride, if you want to, and let him alone."

And so he was called Jim Pride after that. A very nice boy in his ways, he remained so too, in spite of the fearful life around him. And those gamblers of the Minerva Saloon were presently as watchful and jealous of the welfare and morals of this boy as a lover would be of his mistress.

"The boy don't know anything bad, and he ain't going to learn it from you," was the quietus Doc and his revolver put upon the wickedness of more than one too talkative desperado.

"Why don't you set up a Sunday school for the boys here? When me and little Jim takes a hand you will have to call in your checks and close the game, eh, Doc."

From no greater cause than this banter of Joe Bunche, with the laugh of others around the gambling table, came hot words, and then the inevitable revolver. There was in a moment cursing, shooting, yells, and the terrific uproar of a frontier barroom fight. Finally the noise ceased and the crowd came slowly back again. The faro dealer took his seat again.

"Nobody hurt, gentlemen. Now we'll go on with the game!"

It was then that somebody pointed to the corner. A little bunch of clothes lay there behind a chair.

"Oh, God!" Cried the dealer, springing up and throwing away his box and cards. "It's our little boy, Jim. Dead? Yes, dead. And I wish it was me, so help me God! I wish it was me and not him!"

The next day Deadwood had a funeral—a very sad one. There was small coffin into which the entire population in town gazed earnestly and tearfully. Many rough hands, and some cruel hands suddenly became strangely tender and wished to help bear away the coffin.

No one knew the boy's real name; but there was a marble slab at his grave. Was it a tender chord in a gambler's heart that prompted this description?

"Under this bit of turf, under this forest tree
waiting for God to call, lies the pride of the family."

Was the story based on an actual event? Subsequent research has failed to locate, identify, or verify the existence of the story's hero. None of the characters appears in the other newspapers of the day, nor can a Minerva Saloon be found. But perhaps the question in and of itself is moot in that the story may be a parable reflecting what the editor feared was happening in his community, the zeitgeist that defined gold rush camps in the Black Hills at the time.

CHAPTER FIFTEEN

E. B. FARNUM: DEADWOOD'S FIRST MAYOR

Judge of vigilante trials, on the school board, and in Deadwood's first civil government, Farnum did his level best to nurture law and order. Mayor Farnum was elected, along with City Marshal Con Stapleton, in the camp's first vote. He didn't deserve the unsympathetic portrayal that a television series would later bestow.

Mayor E. B. Farnum is perhaps one of the most misrepresented individuals in Deadwood history. Lacking original documents, thanks to the fire of 1879, historians don't even credit the man with being the city's first mayor. This lack of records led David Milch, author of television's *Deadwood* series, to fictionalize Farnum as something that might have been a cross between Gollum and a weasel. Hoping to correct this perception as much as possible, here are the few known facts, most of them gleaned from Deadwood newspapers (especially the *Daily Pioneer* in 1876 and 1877).

Records that exist concerning Ethan Bennett Farnum's life away from Deadwood indicate that he was born sometime around 1828 in Massachusetts. Before coming to Deadwood, Farnum and his wife Mary lived in Wisconsin with their three children; when they arrived in Deadwood, Sylvia was sixteen, Edward twelve, and Lysle two.[1] In 1868, Farnum was the postmaster of Springfield, Wisconsin. Some evidence indicates that this may have been in conjunction with his running a retail store.

E. B. Farnum was perhaps one of the earliest of the non-mining people to arrive in Deadwood Gulch. He promptly opened a hardware store. He was farsighted enough to realize the value of commercial property in Deadwood and secured claims on several Main Street lots, along with those of his business property and his residence on Lower Main Street.[2]

To ensure that solid supply lines were open to Deadwood, Farnum and seven other men financed and promoted the Deadwood-to-Centennial Toll Road project, which was completed in the first week of August 1876. Over this road came the flour, feed, garden seeds, opium, whiskey, nails, saw blades, steam engines, and mining equipment—in short, everything that would be needed to create and maintain a city, including fresh fruit and vegetables.[3] Farnum was a member of the group of businessmen who established the initial value of gold dust, at $16 an ounce, to be used as an instrument of commerce in Deadwood.[4] With the success of his retail business, he went on to invest in several area mining ventures, such as the Laura Mine and the Prince Oscar Lode.[5]

In the earliest days of Deadwood, no official government claimed jurisdiction over the people or the land. For some folks this was an enjoyable situation, for others it was nothing less than an abomination. When James Butler Hickok was shot by Jack McCall, a judge who was seeking his fortune in Deadwood presided over the trial. The outcome of that jury trial so upset Judge Kuykendall, he vowed never again to administer the law in the camp. This one act likely did more to inspire the creation of Deadwood's pro tem government than any other.

When the town chose to install a provisional government, E. B. Farnum was elected as chairman of the first Citizens Committee of Deadwood. Then, on August 18, 1876, an election was held for the town commissioners.[6] Five men were elected, among whom was Sol Star. Young Star had a considerable amount of experience in frontier government, having worked at the Land Office in Helena, Montana Territory, prior to his arrival in the

Dakotas. The committee provided for the construction of a pest house (for isolating folks with communicable diseases), and cleaning streets and alleys.

The office of mayor went to E. B. Farnum, and on September 16, 1876, Judge Whitehead administered the oath of office to Farnum.[7] As mayor, Farnum was very active in efforts to obtain official recognition by the Dakota Territory government and some measure of protection from the U.S. Army. His first act as the official mayor was to draft a letter to General George Crook thanking him for bringing troops to the Black Hills. Enclosed with this letter was a petition signed by Deadwood's citizens, requesting that the army build a fort somewhere near the Black Hills, in order to protect the good people of Deadwood from "the murdering bands of Indians that surround us." Mayor Farnum's letter prompted General Crook to visit the town with a small entourage of army officers in late September 1876.[8]

The next month, Farnum and the commissioners drew up the first city charter, establishing town limits and defining the offices that would manage the government. This document established the mayor's salary at $100 per year, the marshal's pay at $150 per month, and the city clerk's pay at $75 per month. All of the salaries and public maintenance costs were to be defrayed through license fees for various businesses.[9]

While Mayor Farnum was able to send hard copy messages to the outside for help, the *Pioneer* taunted the camp by informing them they were still $5,000 shy of having a working telegraph in their mighty city. One must wonder how self-serving this message to the public was, when all the news the *Pioneer* had arrived by wagon or horseback, or hearsay. Nonetheless, Farnum persevered and, before Christmas, the telegraph was a Deadwood reality.

The first telegraph message from Deadwood was sent by Mayor Farnum asking the army for help against Indian depredations. The years 1876-1877 were tumultuous for both Indians and white settlers and miners. Indians boldly attacked the intruding towns, ranches, and livestock herds. Ranchers and miners in turn stole and sold Indian ponies for $15 a head on a regular basis.[10] Crook City began offering a $50 reward for Indian scalps in June 1877, and Lawrence County followed suit a month later by raising the bounty to $250 for each Indian, dead or alive.[11]

Farnum also was active as the head of the school board, which established the first public school in Deadwood and appointed the ill-fated Mrs. Minnie Callison as its first teacher. Minnie would later become the first and only Deadwood teacher to be bludgeoned to death when she was attacked with a hammer while she slept[12]—even though she kept a small four-barreled Derringer under her pillow.

Farnum also acted as the town's justice of the peace. In November 1876, Justice Farnum performed Deadwood's first "semi-legal" marriage when he joined Fannie Garrettson and "Handsome Banjo Dick" Brown in civil matrimony.[13] Brown and Garretson were a popular musical team in Deadwood who entertained at various saloons and theaters, such as the Gem and the Bella Union. A scant week after the marriage, Fannie and Dick were performing on the stage of the Melodian when a man burst in brandishing an axe. He claimed to be her abandoned husband, and he attempted to kill Dick by throwing the axe at him. Dick stood, pulled his revolver, and fatally shot his assailant. Fannie swore that she and the man, Ed Shaunessey, had never been married, but had lived together for about three years. Dick, of course, was tried for murder and acquitted on self-defense.[14]

Farnum would also act as judge in numerous "trials" for vigilante-captured bad guys. Because his court was not recognized by the territorial government, detainees could not be sentenced to any prison time. Farnum gave only two punishments: freedom or hanging. Horse thieves and cattle rustlers were hanged. Farnum's court was initially conducted over a plank atop two flour kegs, but later he moved to something of an office.

Being exonerated in the Farnum courtroom was often not a blessing, particularly if the local vigilantes did not find the sentence just.

By the time the 1880 federal census rolled around, Farnum must already have decided that he had received his share of Deadwood's gold. He had sold his ranch at the North Water Hole to the Sidney and Black Hills Stage Company and joined his family in Chicago. At age fifty-two, E. B. and his wife, Mary retired. All three of the children were still at home. Edward was working as a printer, his older sister Sylvia worked as a proofreader, and the youngest, Lysle, was still in school.

CHAPTER SIXTEEN

THE FIRST DECADE OF DEADWOOD'S PUBLIC SCHOOLS: 1876-1886

This chapter is dedicated to the memory of Deadwood's first public school teacher, Mrs. Minnie Callison, who taught school in Deadwood from 1877 to 1878. Murdered in her bed, Minnie was buried with a wooden grave marker in Deadwood's Mount Moriah Cemetery.

Surely something as important as education has been to the residents of Deadwood through the course of the town's history has been well re-corded and re-recorded. Just as surely, that history was likely "sanitized," not so much through blatant lies as by simple omissions. On the other hand, the following timeline of education-related events is the version that was familiar to every Deadwood resident who could read between 1876 and 1886. It was part of the ongoing stream of news that hit Deadwood's streets through the *Black Hills Pioneer* and the *Black Hills Times*, but writers of Deadwood's school history would chose to ignore this decade.

Primary Education

Deadwood residents began thinking about schools early on. In 1876, the sixth issue of Deadwood's first newspaper[1] made a brief statement on the state of public education at the time. In one sentence on the back page, just below the announcement that Calamity Jane was now in Cheyenne, the editor noted that there seemed to be enough "little ones" around the gulches to justify organizing a school.

Prediction, request, or command, who can say? Two weeks later, concerned citizens met to establish a school board and to set up boundaries for the first school district. After William DeMoss agreed to serve as pro tem president and William Hollins as secretary, a board of directors was elected. Dr. McKinney became president; E. B. Farnum, treasurer; and William Hollins, secretary. The directors were then instructed to canvass and solicit subscriptions to defray the cost of the school and to select and hire a competent teacher, while securing a suitable building.

In the same issue, the paper applauded the efforts of electing a school board and establishing guidelines and goals for it. The editor cited lack of an educational system as a culprit that robs towns of larger populations, because workers had to support their families elsewhere in order to provide good educational opportunities.

The folks of Deadwood were serious. In early September they sent a representative east to procure samples of the day's textbooks and send them back for approval. That is not to say that there were no problems, for there were many. Subscriptions for $80 a month had been obtained, but nothing was being done with the money. The critics at the *Pioneer* thought membership changes in the board might solve many of the problems. The editorial went on to demand that Deadwood's children be properly educated and prepared for the "great battle of life." Without such training the children "would be doomed to be mere machines of labor through blighted lives, without hope of ameliorating their condition."

Apparently the editorial had its effect on the elected movers and shakers, because in two weeks a teacher was produced, one Mr. E. Kermode, and Tom Miller (owner of the Bella Union) loaned the district a house on Third Street to use as a school building. The teacher was noted in two November issues of the weekly *Pioneer* as having occupied the school and

As rough and tumble as Deadwood was, its citizens cherished their children and enthusiastically supported efforts to educate them.

was preparing to begin teaching on the 20th. The 20th came and went, but there was no documented celebration for the establishment of a school. It seemed as though the teacher never taught.

Thus it came to pass that the private schools superseded the public schools in the young town, when Mrs. D. T. Smith ran an advertisement in the *Pioneer* announcing that she would be opening a "select school" in December 1876. The same ad stated she would be charging $1.25 per week for each scholar. The *Pioneer* ran a short but flattering article boasting that her accomplishments were of a superior order and that she was sure to be successful in her endeavor. The paper did, however, fail to note the exact nature of her accomplishments or where she had performed them.

But where did that leave Deadwood in its quest for a public school? Still looking for a teacher. By early January one had been found, the wife of a miner who was then prospecting near Keystone. Her name was Minnie Callison. She had the formal education for the job, and also the backing of Mayor E. B. Farnum, Dr. Babcock, and a number of other prominent businessmen. She started her school immediately, and as the school year went on, the *Pioneer* noted in February that she had twenty-seven students. In addition to her education and abilities, Mrs. Callison had other attractions: she was slight of build, 5 feet 4 inches tall, with black hair and black eyes that commanded attention in whatever room she entered. By May 1878, eighty-seven students attended the school and the board of education hired a second teacher, Miss Ida Snyder.

Mrs. Callison made it through the three months of her initial contract with flying colors; her contract was renewed to the end of the year, and then renewed for the entire year of 1878. But summer vacation would prove to be her demise. It was common knowledge that Minnie had several ardent male admirers in the camp, a fact that was mostly overlooked because of her extreme value to the process of turning Deadwood into a town as opposed to just another "here today gone tomorrow" mining camp. But on the morning of August 17, 1878, the camp's pretty young teacher lay dead on her bed in a pool of blood. Her forehead appeared to have received at least seven to nine blows from a blunt instrument such as a hammer.

When the coroner continued his examination of the scene, he noted that Deadwood's first school teacher slept with a small, four-barreled

Derringer. Did she feel the need for a gun because her husband was working in Keystone, or because she had reason to think she was in harm's way, or was it a straightforward response to Deadwood's ambient social environment? After Minnie Callison's death and the murder trial that followed, the primary school teachers produced only a scattering of smaller scandals and limited themselves to much lesser sins, such as the teacher who decided reading pocket novels (starring Deadwood Dick?) to the students equaled a good lesson in American literature. After she shined the light of contemporary pulp fiction on the children but a scant few times, the parents complained, nearly creating an uprising. The idea of a real school in a "blood and guts" mining camp had a tendency to make the rest of America snicker, as evidenced in an article from the New Orleans' *Times-Picayune* that reported "A strange female who landed in Deadwood the other day to start a pretty girl-waiter saloon, was induced by liberal offers to forgo her intentions and become the principal of the First Ward School.[3]

A High School for Deadwood

With a few years of mostly smooth teaching under its belt, Deadwood began to feel the need for a high school. The wealthier families of the community, such as Judge Moody's, had been sending their promising children to Yankton and even farther for their high school needs. These needs found expression in an editorial in the *Black Hills Daily Times* in October 1880, which read in part, "We desire to see such a school in Deadwood—a school where young ladies and gentlemen may be fitted for the higher institutions of learning."

By the fall of 1881, the hope for a high school took tangible form, and by the end of December, a new high school was turned over to the board of education. In January 1882, the Deadwood School Board held its first meeting of the New Year there. William Carey, president of the Deadwood Board of Education, invited all residents of Deadwood who were "concerned about the success of Deadwood's schools, to meet with the School Board at the new High School." Lawrence County announced that it now had forty-five school districts. The following month, the high school discovered a need for music instruction, so the superintendent of schools, Mr.

Deadwood's first high school, a two-story wood-frame building, sat in the floodplain of Whitewood Creek on the south end of town.

J. K. Davis, ran an ad in the *Times* asking for someone to rent an organ to the high school. He promised that it would receive the best of care and, in the event that damage should occur, the school board would pay for it.

Final touches were put on the high school yard when Patrick Early flooded it, then graded it. They may not have had a gymnasium, but they did have a first-rate playground. The editor of the *Times* thought "The yard is one of the finest play grounds in the Territory and the sight of it is enough to make him wish he was a boy again."

All things considered, everyone with concerns for Deadwood's schools was pretty satisfied with the forward direction of education in the town, but no one was ready for what happened next.

In late February 1883, the first inkling of a problem occurred when Whitewood Creek in South Deadwood left its banks and began spreading toward the new high school. But this was just the harbinger of dire times to come. The winter of 1882-1883 had been extra harsh, with very little thawing. The snow load in places became more than 10 feet thick. No one really seemed alarmed until the melt began.

On the morning of May 17, 1883, it was noted that Whitewood Creek had once again risen over its banks and was spreading across the lower levels of the gulch. The alarm was spread by telephone from Ten Mile Ranch. This ignited the fears of many, who started moving their belongings, animals, and school books to higher ground, but the new high school, which cost $12,000 to build, "the pride of the city" with its furniture, maps and charts, disappeared in the deluge. Most folks thought that by morning the worst of it would have passed, but May 18th came and went with the flood in full fury, carrying away of hundreds of homes, barns, businesses, saloons, and churches. (The corner-stone of that first high school is on display at the Mount Moriah Cemetery gift shop. It should be noticed that the stone had a pocket in its center to serve as a "time capsule," the contents of which vanished downstream on that fateful day.) With many of the telephone poles and wires sullied or destroyed by the flood, communications between Deadwood and South Deadwood had been reduced to a rope and basket strung across the torrent.

Reconstruction

When the mud and the bodies settled, it was not long before whiskey was being sold across a bar suspended over two barrels. Boards were being cut and bricks fired, and Deadwood did what it has always done best in the face of disaster: regenerate a new, more vibrant city and a sustaining economy. Land was found for a new high school in July, and a contract to build the new school was awarded to Kid and Benn. In August 1883, surveyors put stakes in the ground to identify the property boundaries. That same month, masons finished laying the foundation for the building. According to the *Times*, S. F. Jacoby cut the stone caps, sills, and downspouts for the new school, and 150,000 bricks were fired to raise it.[4]

The first-ward school bell was moved to the high school and placed in position on November 28, 1883, and its clear notes rang out for the first time from its final post of duty. The bell carried a very fine tone and proved satisfactory to those in charge. The official opinion of the *Times* was "The first ward school bell replaced the demoralized noise producer at the [new] high school building," but of course it had taken the paper several weeks to notice. The "new" school bell in the tower of new high school building was also to be used by the Methodist Church to announce beginning of services. On January 6, 1884, the school board accepted the new school and even went so far as to hire a permanent janitor, Mr. Ayers, who was to receive $30 a month for his services.

The second school was an exact duplicate of the one washed away in the flood except that it was located on Main Street facing southeast, and the foundation was twenty-five feet above the street level. In other words, if the new school was taken out by another flood, the entire town would be gone too. (Before the flood of 1883, the new high school and the Methodist Church were next to each other near the present location of the Slime Plant (now part of the Deadwood Mountain Grand Resort). After the flood, the school was rebuilt on the northern slope of the gulch facing Main Street. The Methodist Church was built a few hundred feet northeast of the high school on Williams Street.)

In March 1884, the school board resolved that Professor L. L. Conant would be given complete and total control of the Deadwood school system. Then on July 8, 1884, the city decided that the new high school was not large enough, and a contract for a school addition was awarded to Damon, Barker and Evans. On August 3, 1884, the brick work was completed on this addition.

During the following July, the school board made a decision that polarized the residents of Deadwood against them, by firing the superintendent, Professor Conant, without stating a reason. Conant had the trust of the public and had endeared himself to the upper crust of Deadwood society. (He went on to teach math at the Dakota School of Mines, then returned to his native Massachusetts for a career as math professor at the Worcester Polytechnic Institute.)

On the day following that decision, the *Times* argued that all of the taxpayers and parents of Deadwood thought poorly of the school board's decision to dismiss Professor Conant and replace him with a complete stranger, who had no experience with the Deadwood school system. The editorial ended with a statement that it was the citizens

Deadwood High School as it looked in 1909.

who paid for the maintenance of the schools, and their wishes were entitled to respectful consideration.

On July 9, forty-eight of Deadwood's leading citizens published their signatures on a petition for a public meeting concerning the dismissal of Professor Conant. The following day, the meeting occurred at the courthouse, chaired by Judge Bennett and attended by about fifty citizens. A secretary was appointed and a committee assigned to draw up a document stating why it was wrong for the school board to have fired Professor Conant, and why he should be immediately rehired. The committee was composed of Messrs. Raymond, Lincoln, Van Cise, Kingsley, and Babcock. They went to work and quickly produced a document complete with a preamble and four resolutions. The document was read aloud and met group approval. Then Judge Kingsley took the floor and gave an impassioned speech as to why the resolutions should be adopted.

When Kingsley had finished, the floor was turned over to Judge McLaughlin. McLaughlin called for some light and then began to unwrap a large bulky package that contained the laws governing the school board, along with a number of testimonies attesting to the good character and abilities of Mr. Free, the person hired to replace Professor Conant. McLaughlin went on to inform the assembly that a legal and binding contract had already been entered into between the Board of Education and Mr. Free, and it could not be legally broken without Mr. Free's consent. McLaughlin then proceeded to outline the reason for Professor Conant's dismissal, which included a pronounced lack of organizational skills. He concluded his elucidation by saying that even if Mr. Free chose not to accept the position, the board would not consider a new application by Professor Conant.

A number of speakers followed Judge McLaughlin, all of whom supported Professor Conant. Be that as it may, in the end the vote rejected the resolutions supporting retention of Professor Conant by twenty-one to thirty. The Deadwood education system had now come full circle. It had survived fire, flood, and social unrest, and was finally ready to present a finished product: its first graduating high school class.

The Accomplished Six

The first Deadwood High School graduation occurred June 28, 1886, and consisted entirely of young ladies, six to be exact: Miss Annette Forest, Miss Belle Chase, Miss Estelline Bennett, Miss Irene Cushman, Miss Mamie Phillips, and Miss Minnie Craig. During that school year, senior class attendance was 92.3 percent, punctuality was 98.3 percent, and the percentage of progress was 93.3.

The ceremonies were conducted in the Opera House, where lighting was provided by two electric lamps suspended from the auditorium's ceiling. The graduating class was seated beneath a suspended evergreen colored sign that read: "Not Who, but What - 1886"

The South Deadwood Hose Company presented each of the girls a bouquet or basket of flowers. Immediately behind the graduates sat the School Board, Mayor Sol Star, judges, and other local dignitaries.

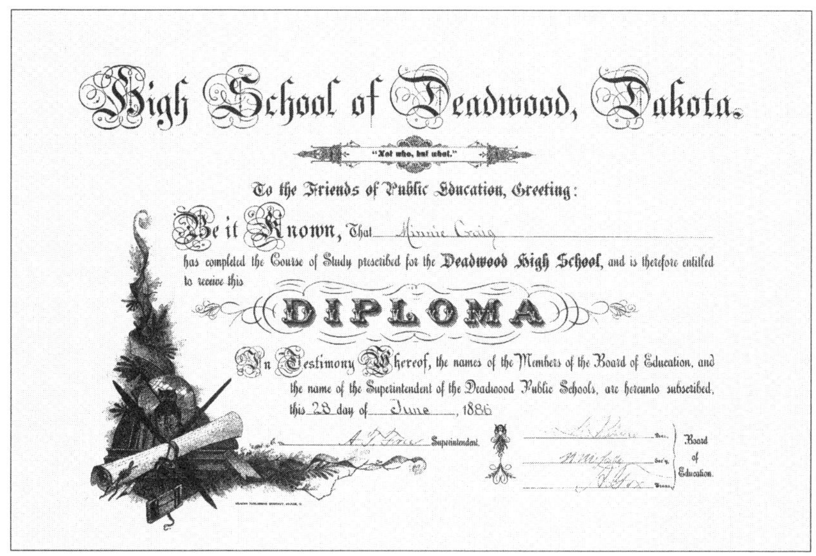

High School of Deadwood, Dakota.

"Not who, but what."

To the Friends of Public Education, Greeting:

Be it Known, That Minnie Craig

has completed the Course of Study prescribed for the Deadwood High School, and is therefore entitled to receive this

DIPLOMA

In Testimony Whereof, the names of the Members of the Board of Education, and the name of the Superintendent of the Deadwood Public Schools, are hereunto subscribed, this 28 day of June, 1886

A. J. [illegible] Superintendent.

[illegible] Pres.
[illegible] Sec'y.
[illegible] Treas.

Board of Education.

Minnie Craig was one of six among Deadwood High's first graduating class in 1886.

The evening began with an overture by the Deadwood Band, followed by a prayer delivered by Mr. John Fairbank (a local member of the fraternal organization, the Grand Army of the Republic). A quartet sang "Come Where the Lilies Bloom," then each member of the graduating class gave an oration on her particular subject. The editor of the *Times* complained bitterly about the Opera House's poor acoustics, stating that was why he did not have a better report of the orations. He nevertheless thought the deliveries were excellent.

In the middle of the six oratories, Miss Lulu Kingsley played Liszt's "Miserere du Trovatore" on the piano. For her playing she received loud applause and a "perfect avalanche of flowers." Mr. D. A. McPherson delivered the closing remarks from the school board, and the president of the school board gave awards to the graduates.

The *Times* editor praised Professor Free and all the teachers under his direction for the quality of work in producing such a promising group of graduates and noted that the next year's graduates would include some boys, but they would have to work and study very hard to match the Class of '86.

In September 1886, two of the young ladies mentioned in the graduation ceremonies of 1886 boarded a stagecoach bound east to further their education. One was Miss Estelline Bennett and the other, the graduation pianist, Miss Lulu Kingsley. Both were headed to Elmira, New York, to study at the women's school, Elmira College, for a year. Both girls returned to Deadwood in June 1887 for the summer. The *Times* reported them in excellent health and delighted to be home.

In May 1887, another of the "Accomplished Six," Irene Cushman, opened a kindergarten in Deadwood. In the fall, Miss Cushman traveled to Boston to continue her education, while the Misses Kingsley and Bennett returned to Elmira. Miss Kingsley would then go on to the Boston Conservatory for Music to study piano and voice, and eventually move to Denver with her parents; Miss Bennett would return to the Hills and eventually write the classic Deadwood history, *Old Deadwood Days*. In October 1891, Irene Cushman married Albert Wilson. The wedding guest list read like the upper crust of "who's who" in Deadwood.

Beginning in 1889, Mamie Phillips taught school for a while in Nevada.

A sense of accomplishment radiates from this unidentified woman with her diploma. In the late 1800s, about half of all youth aged 5 to 19 were enrolled in school, and even as late as 1940, more than half of all students dropped out by eighth grade.

During summers, she traveled, accompanied by her mother, but by 1897 Miss Phillips was back home, teaching in Deadwood. After the turn of the century, she taught in Hot Springs, South Dakota.

Minnie Craig married George Felix Ingram on Christmas the year following her graduation. She and George raised a family in Helena, Montana.

Following her graduation, Annette Forest married Joseph Gandolfo in 1888. They remained in Deadwood until at least 1910, where they raised two boys, Forest and Melvin.

No camp, no village, no city or metropolis could have asked for a better product than the first graduating class of Deadwood High.

CHAPTER SEVENTEEN

THE TELEPHONE COMES TO DEADWOOD

Deadwood was pretty tickled to be in the forefront of U.S. telephone usage, but even civic-pride bragging was subject to the barbs two newspapers aimed constantly at each other.

When Alexander Graham Bell invented and patented the telephone in 1876, Deadwood had just begun publishing its first newspaper, the *Black Hills Pioneer,* and it was December that year before the first telegraph lines connected Deadwood to the rest of the world. Another year passed before the first mention of the telephone appeared in a Black Hills newspaper; and this was merely a comparison of the telephone and the phonograph. The *Black Hills Champion* editor opined that Edison's phonograph was a much more wonderful invention than Bell's telephone. A scant four months later, the first telephones were installed in the Black Hills.

Initially, there were only two telephones: one in the office of the *Black Hills Pioneer*, and one in the office of its competitor, the *Black Hills Times*. Wires were strung between the two offices and then they waited!

Wall-mounted telephones like this one featured a hand-cranked magneto that generated an electrical current to ring a switchboard operator who would then connect the call.

The fledgling telephone company had forgotten to order telephone-pole wire insulators, but on March 9, 1878, the lines were completed and staff of the two rival offices held their first telephone conversation.[1]

After that, the invention spread like a virus. In June 1879, the *Times* ran an editorial stating that telephone equipment was becoming cheaper than dirt, and that the telephone craze was raging among the women folk. In the fall of 1879, soon after the Great Fire of '79, there was talk about town of connecting a fire alarm system to the telephone system. Meanwhile, the Homestake Mine in nearby Lead began putting up lines for its own phone system. In December 1880, the last telephone lines were strung between Lead and Central City, connecting all the camps of the Northern Hills. Lines were also rapidly approaching Spearfish. The *Black Hills Daily Times* noted in January 1881 that it could not exist without the telephone. Thus, in a few short years Bell's invention had captivated the residents of the Black Hills.

In the journalistic style of the day, Deadwood's newspapers kept up a continual feud, regularly zinging insults at the other, in print. The *Black Hills Weekly Pioneer* was the elder, its first small issue released by W. A. Laughlin and A. W. Merrick on June 8, 1876. Ten months later, Porter Warner's *Deadwood Daily Times* began on April 7. (In 1897, the two would combine as the *Pioneer-Times.*) The *Times,* with forethought and humor, recalled the gist of Deadwood's first telephone conversation between the two newspapers:

Tel-e-phon-e-story

> *It is already pretty well understood that we have a telephone; i.e., we have one end of it. The* Pioneer *has the other. And we are tolerably well convinced also that this is a big thing, and that a brief statement of its merits and peculiarities would be just the thing at this time. But we desire to remark in the onset, that this wonderful little contrivance is not yet in good working order, owing to the absence of insulators. This difficulty, however, will soon be obviated. Mr. Halley, the general supervisor of the line, intends getting up some "homemade" insulators which will do the business. We cannot spare the space sufficient to give a description of the machine. All the men who are curious in this regard have our consent to drop in at the* Pioneer *office and interview that little sinner in the most racketous manner, and with their accustomed levity. But the ladies may call at this office and satisfy their curiosity. They will at all times find our Professor present, ready to teach them its modus operandi. And then besides, ours is a lady's 'phony. It is the moral part of the outfit. The* Pioneer's *little kuss is profane, sometimes. Ours never got off wrong but once, and that is when one gang from*

the other end got hold of it. Notwithstanding the moral character of telephone, we are actuated by our little hatchet characteristics to confess that it is to some extent a promoter of intemperance and profanity. This is evidently owing to its forced connection with the demoralized one [the Pioneer*] on Sherman Street. To illustrate we subjoin a batch of questions, answers and conundrums spoken during the first half hour of its [existence] in the Hills.*

A well-known citizen was the first to tackle it, and it was probably owing to the example he set which caused the demoralization that followed. "Hello?" was his first explanation. No reply. It was repeated and the sinner on the other end omitted the "o" in receiving it, and answered, "You go there yourself and pump thunder for grub, you old rooster!" "Come down here and take a drink." "All right." "Meet me at the corner;" and they met and smiled. Then another sinner opened up at the Sherman Street end. The gentleman at our "'phony" requested him to proceed with his racket, and a still small voice, like the soft horns of Elf-land faintly blowing, said, "Go to h—l!" Then a wicked man who happened to slip in unobserved, went back after the profane fish at the Pioneer *headquarters; "What der yer soy?" "Come on down and take a little fire-water." "Be jabbers an' I'll do it," and he skipped out in great haste. Next the boss fabricator of the* Pioneer *tried his luck, and knowing the* Times *corps would entertain nothing but a truthful exchange of compliments, etc., he turned loose with a strange mixture of facts, which so astonished and confused their little joker—it not being prepared for it—that it utterly refused to transmit a single sound. But when he said "Come down and I'll treat," the words were conveyed very distinctly, because they had "no foundation in truth." Now a doctor engaged the attention of the machine. He propounded a conundrum, in hopes of changing the immoral current of the little villains. Accordingly he asked, "What was the greatest freak of nature than the birth of Siamese twins?" "Give it up!" "Why, Mary had a little lamb." This brought both ends of the house down, and instead of lessening the current of immorality, everybody said, "It's d—m good; let's go have a drink on that." Everybody fell in but us.*

The reader can draw his own inferences from the above sample specimens as to the manner of beast the telephone is.

After getting rid of the sinful men above quoted, experiments were made with a flute, a music box, and the alarm of a clock, and they worked like a charm. The words and the melody of songs were transmitted with remarkable distinctness. The voices of the singers were even distinguishable, and the cadence was softened and rendered more mellifluent by its transmission.

No. Deadwood D. T. April 1st 1883

Received of California Mfg Co

For Exchange Rent to May 1st — $ 10

For 1 $ instruments — 5

For

For

Received Payment, Total

Black Hills Telephone Exchange

Per Paul Newman

Times Printing House.

This receipt for a month's services from the Black Hills Telephone Exchange dates from April 1883.

Postscript

During the Great Flood of 1883, Whitewood Creek rose up from its banks and swept half the town away, including the new high school. Lives were lost during that violent spring melt, but it could have been far, far worse if the progress of the melt and the creek's rise had not been reported by observers along the telephone line until the poles and lines fell in the deluge.

CHAPTER EIGHTEEN

THE LOCOMOTIVE *J. B. HAGGIN*

The Haggin was the first locomotive operating in the Deadwood area, and it served until 1900. Today this survivor awaits visitors to the Adams Museum.

On August 20, 1879, the first steam locomotive to enter the Black Hills was hauled down Deadwood's Main Street on wagons pulled by oxen. Christened the *J. B. Haggin*, this five-ton, 22-inch-gauge wood-burner was capable of hauling fifteen ore cars or thirty tons of ore. The locomotive was named after James Ben Ali Haggin, a Kentucky-born partner in the company that owned and operated the Homestake Mine.

This sturdy little engine hauled ore at the Homestake from 1879 to 1900 when it was replaced by compressed air locomotives. The *Haggin* was one of three identical engines. The other two locomotives were named the *I. C. Stump* and the *W. R. Hearst*. Of the three Baldwin locomotives, the *Haggin* is the only one known to still exist. After being retired, the *Haggin* was polished, placed in storage at the Homestake, and brought out only for special occasions. On January 15, 1932, the small engine went on permanent loan to the Adams Museum. A portion of the museum's

The J. B. Haggin *at work at the Homestake Mine.*

back wall was removed, and tracks were laid into the building. The *J. B. Haggin*'s boiler was filled with compressed air and she rode into the museum (where she still resides) under her own power.[1]

And now, a bit more about the locomotive's namesake. In 1850, James Ben Ali Haggin opened a law office with Lloyd Tevis in Sacramento, California, later moving to San Francisco. He soon invested in a mining venture with George Hearst (whose son, William Randolph Hearst, was destined to be a newspaper tycoon), and the business grew to become one of the largest mining companies in the United States, operating the Anaconda Copper Mine with Marcus Daly in Butte, Montana, the Ontario silver mine near Park City, Utah, and other properties.

The J. B. Haggin *at home in the Adams Museum in Deadwood.* COURTESY DEADWOOD HISTORY, INC., DEADWOOD, SD.

BIBLIOGRAPHY

All illustrations are from the collection of Jerry L. Bryant unless otherwise credited.

Newspapers and Documents

Atchison Daily Globe (Kansas)

Atlanta Constitution (Georgia)

Bismarck Tribune (Dakota Territory)

Black Hills Champion (Deadwood)

Black Hills Daily Times (Deadwood)

Black Hills Weekly Times (Deadwood)

Black Hills Weekly Pioneer (Deadwood)

Black Hills Weekly Pioneer Mining Review (Deadwood)

Burlington Hawk Eye (Iowa)

Cheyenne Daily Leader (Wyoming)

Colorado Weekly Chieftain (Pueblo, CO)

Colored Troops Military Service Records, 1861-1865. National Archives, Washington, DC

Daily Evening Free Press (Pierre, Dakota Territory)

Daily Northwestern (Oshkosh, Wisconsin)

Dakota Journal (Pierre, Dakota Territory)

Dakota Register (Chamberlain, Dakota Territory)

Deadwood Daily Times

Daily Pioneer (Deadwood)

Grand Forks Herald (North Dakota)

Inter Ocean (Chicago, IL)

Lincoln Evening News (Nebraska)

Mitchell Daily Republican (Dakota Territory)

Mitchell Times Republican (Dakota Territory)

Nebraska State Journal (Lincoln, NE)

Omaha Daily Bee (Nebraska)

Omaha World Herald (Nebraska)

Pioneer Times (Deadwood)

Queen City Weekly Times (Spearfish, South Dakota)

Rare Bargains in Cynthia E. Cleveland's Addition to Highmore, Dakota. Advertising flyer. Archives of South Dakota State Historical Society, Pierre.

Rocky Mountain News (Denver, CO)

Salt Lake City Tribune (Utah)

Stevens Point Gazette (Wisconsin)

Traverse City Herald (Michigan)

Vancouver Daily World (British Columbia, Canada)

Washington Post (Washington DC)

Books

Bennett, Estelline. *Old Deadwood Days.*

2nd ed. New York: *Charles Scribner's Sons,* 1935.

Casey, Robert. *The Black Hills.* Indianapolis: Bobbs-Merrill Co., 1949.

Cleveland, Cynthia E. *His Honor or, Fate's Mysteries.* New York: The American News Company, 1890.

Cleveland, Cynthia. *See-Saw.* University of Michigan Library, January 1, 1887.

Herringshaw, Thomas William. *Herringshaw's Encyclopedia of American Biography.* Chicago: American Publishers' Association, 1914.

Kuykendall, William L. *Frontier Days.* Denver: J. M. and H. L. Kuykendall, 1917.

Johnson, Rossiter. *Twentieth Century Biographical Dictionary of Notable Americans.* Vol. II. Rare Books Com, 2012.

Interviews/correspondence

Abebe, Tewodros. Senior Archivist.

Howard University. Washington, DC.

Karl, Jamie. Administrative Director. Oakland County Pioneer and Historical Society. Pontiac, Michigan.

Lem-Sharp, Judy. Librarian. U.S. Treasury Department. Washington, DC.

ENDNOTES

Chapter 1 – Before Deadwood: People Come and Gone

1. *Black Hills Pioneer*, June 17, 1876.
2. *Black Hills Pioneer*, August 26, 1876.
3. *Black Hills Daily Times*, July 17, 1877.
4. *Daily Times*, May 8, 1878.
5. *Daily Times*, May 30, 1878.
6. *Daily Times*, June 8, 1878.
7. *Daily Times*, June 17, 1878.
8. *Pioneer*, June 18, 1878.
9. *Daily Times*, June 12, 1890.

Chapter 2 – A Trip Down the Gulch with Barker, the Black Hills Hermit

1. *Black Hills Champion*, July 8, 1877.

Chapter 3 – Adrienne Davis: A Woman among the Miners

1. *New York Daily Graphic*, August 24, 1877.
2. *Graphic*, September 15, 1877.
3. *Graphic*, October 5, 1877.
4. *Graphic*, October 30, 1877.
5. *Graphic*, February 28, 1878.

Chapter 4 – Chambers C. Davis: The Brief Life of Deadwood's First Assayer

1. *Denver Daily Times, May 13, 1874.*
2. (Golden) *Colorado Transcript, April 5, 1876.*
3. *Black Hills Times, May 26, 1877.*
4. *Black Hills Times, July 7, 1877.*
5. *Black Hills Daily Times, June 17, 1878.*
6. *Black Hills Times, April 7, 1879.*
7. *Black Hills Times, April 7, 1879*
8. *Black Hills Pioneer, April 11, 1879.*
9. *Black Hills Times, April 24, 1879.*

Chapter 5 – Con Stapleton: Deadwood's First Marshal

1. *Black Hills Pioneer*, September 16, 1876.

Chapter 6 – Sarah Ann Erb: Madam of the Bulldog Ranches

1. *Black Hills Times*, November 12, 1877.
2. *Black Hills Daily Times*, July 13, 1879.
3. *Daily Times*, January 6, 1880.

4. *Daily Times*, December 12, 1878.
5. *Daily Times*, February 27, 1880.
6. *Daily Times*, September 26, 1878.
7. *Daily Times*, August 5, 1879; August 6, 1879.
8. Ten Mile Ranch was located in the same small valley as the town of Englewood, but on the opposite side of the valley, as was the Englewood School. The hills on this side of the valley were also host to a multitude of mining explorations still visible today.
9. *Daily Times*, August 6, 1879.
10. *Daily Times*, August 7, 1870; August 13, 1879.
11. *Daily Times*, August 14, 1879.
12. *Daily Times*, August 16, 1879; September 19, 1879.
13. *Daily Times*, November 13, 1878; *Black Hills Daily Pioneer*, October 11, 1878; *Black Hills Daily Times*, May 19, September 2, 1880; 1880 U.S. Census, National Archive Film T9-0113, p. 321A; *Daily Times*, May 7, 1877.
14. *Daily Times*, September 4, 1880.
15. *Daily Times*, September 8, 1880.
16. *Daily Times*, September 24, 1880.
17. *Daily Times*, September 26, 1880.
18. *Daily Times*, September 29, 1880.
19. *Daily Times*, October 9, 1880.
20. *Daily Times*, November 6, December 1, 19, 22, 29, 1880.
21. *Daily Times*, January 19, 1881.
22. *Daily Times*, January 6, 1882.
23. *Daily Times*, February 8, 1882.
24. *Daily Times*, March 9, 1882.
25. *Daily Times*, June 7, 1882; October 14, 1879; February 22, 1883.
26. *Daily Times*, March 4, 1882.
27. *Daily Times*, March 6, 1882.
28. *Daily Times*, March 20, 1882.
29. *Daily Times*, August 31, 1882.
30. *Daily Times*, December 31, 1889.

Chapter 7 – Mollie Johnson: Queen of the Blondes

1. *Black Hills Daily Times*, August 27, 1879.
2. *Daily Times*, July 18, 1879.

Chapter 8 – Elizabeth Lovell: Amazon of Elizabethtown

1. *Black Hills Daily Times*, September 19, 1877.
2. *Black Hills Daily Pioneer*, January 16, 1878.
3. *Daily Pioneer*, January 16, 1878.
4. *Daily Pioneer*, April 27, 1878.
5. *Black Hills Daily Times*, May 7, 1878.
6. *Daily Times*, June 25 1878.
7. *Daily Times*, June 26, 1878.
8. *Daily Times*, June 27, 1878.
9. A search of the Deadwood Historical Newspaper database returns 699 hits on the name Hastie between April 1877 and July 1887. It appears he was born in Ireland and educated in Illinois. He initially became a partner of Judge Joe Miller in 1877, and by November 1878 had been elected as district attorney.
10. *Daily Times*, June 28, 1878.
11. *Daily Times*, July 29, 1878.
12. *Daily Times*, July 30, 1878.
13. *Black Hills Daily Pioneer*, October 11, 1878.
14. *Daily Pioneer*, October 11, 1878.
15. *Black Hills Daily Times*, April 14, 1879.
16. *Daily Times*, October 14, 1878.
17. *Black Hills Daily Pioneer*, June 18, 1878.
18. *Black Hills Daily Times*, April 14, 1879.
19. *Daily Times*, December 29, 1881.
20. *Daily Times*, July 1, 1879.
21. *Daily Times*, April 22, 1879.
22. *Daily Times*, April 18, 1879.
23. *La Crosse* (Wisconsin) *Tribune*, August 20, 1908; *Aberdeen* (South Dakota) *American*, August 21, 1908.

Chapter 9 – Justin Cachlin: Frenchy the Bottle Fiend

1. *Black Hills Daily Times*, November 4, 5, 1879.
2. *Daily Times*, May 14, 1877.
3. *Daily Times*, June 5, 1877.
4. *Daily Times*, March 9, 1878.
5. *Daily Times*, July 18, 1878.

6. *Daily Times*, June 28, 1879.
7. *Daily Times*, February 22, 1880.
8. *Daily Times*, August 23, 1878.
9. *Daily Times*, March 19, 1878.
10. *Daily Times*, April 8, 1878.
11. *Daily Times*, March 29, 1879.
12. *Daily Times*, June 28, 1879.
13. *Bismarck Tribune*, January 16, 1880.
14. *Black Hills Weekly Pioneer*, March 6, 1880.
15. *Black Hills Pioneer*, March 27, 1880.
16. *Black Hills Daily Times*, December 7, 1881.
17. *Bismarck Tribune*, December 10, 1881.
18. *Black Hills Daily Times*, January 9, 1881.
19. *Black Hills Daily Times*, February 17, 1882.

Chapter 10 – Henrico Livingstone: Obstructionist Extraordinaire

1. Robert Casey, *The Black Hills* (Indianapolis: Bobbs Merrill, 1949), p. 143.
2. Estelline Bennett, *Old Deadwood Days* (2nd ed., New York: Charles Scribner's Sons, 1935), p. 3.
3. U.S. Census, 1880 and 1900, Lawrence County, Dakota Territory and South Dakota.
4. *Black Hills Pioneer Times*, January 11, 1910.
5. (Lincoln) *Nebraska State Journal*, January 13, 1910; *Grand Forks* (North Dakota) *Herald*, January 14, 1910.
6. *Black Hills Champion*, August 6, 1877.
7. *Champion*, December 23, 1877.
8. *Black Hills Daily Times*, October 1, 1882; November 1, 1882; December 2, 1882.
9. *Daily Times*, March 4, 1883.
10. *Daily Times*, June 20, 1883; July 6, 1883; August 11, 1883; August 15, 1883.
11. *Black Hills Daily Pioneer*, September 3, 1885.
12. *Daily Times*, September 13, 1885.
13. *Daily Times*, January 5, 1886.
14. *Daily Times*, January 22, 1886.
15. *Daily Times*, January 23, 1886.
16. *Daily Times*, May 23, 1886.
17. *Daily Times*, September 22, 1886.

18. *Daily Times*, October 8, 1886.
19. *Daily Times*, March 11, 1887; March 12, 1887.
20. *Daily Times*, April 20, 1887.
21. *Daily Times*, May 18, 1887.
22. *Daily Times*, April 17, 1888.
23. *Daily Times*, April 18, 1888.
24. *Daily Times*, April 25, 1888.
25. *Daily Times*, May 3, 1888.
26. *Daily Times*, October 6, 1889.
27. *Daily Times*, November 2, 1889.
28. *Lincoln* (Nebraska) *Evening News*, July 29, 1891.
29. *Black Hills Daily Times*, August 1, 1891.
30. *Daily Times*, August 4, 1891.
31. *Daily Times*, August 11, 1891; *Omaha World Herald*, August 13, 1891.
32. *Daily Times*, August 12, 1891.
33. *Daily Times*, August 15, 1891.
34. *Black Hills Pioneer Times*, January 11, 1910; *Nebraska State Journal*, January 13, 1910; *Grand Forks Herald*, January 14, 1910.

Chapter 11 – General Samuel Fields: Political Aspirant

1. United States Federal Census of 1900, Omaha, Nebraska.
2. U.S., Colored Troops Military Service Records, 1861-1865 Record for Samuel Fields, National Archives, Washington, D.C.
3. United States Census 1870, Third Ward, La Fourche County, p. 46.
4. *Omaha World Herald*, July 1, 1903.
5. *Rocky Mountain News*, January 14, 1874.
6. *Rocky Mountain Daily News*, September 1, 1874.
7. *Rocky Mountain News*, September 2, 1874.
8. (Pueblo, Colorado) *Weekly Chieftain*, September 3, 1874.
9. *Rocky Mountain News*, January 20, 1875.
10. *Denver Daily Times*, February 25, 1875.
11. *Rocky Mountain News*, April 16, 1875.
12. William L. Kuykendall, *Frontier Days* (Denver: J. M. and H. L. Kuykendall, 1917), pp. 234-235.
13. *Cheyenne Daily Leader*, July 23, 1876.
14. *Black Hills Daily Pioneer*, July 12, 1876.

15. *Black Hills Daily Times*, March 27 1878.
16. United States Census of 1900, Omaha, Nebraska.
17. *Burlington* (Iowa) *Daily Hawk-Eye*, June 16, 1876.
18. *Black Hills Champion*, August 6, 1877.
19. *Champion*, December 30, 1877.
20. *Black Hills Daily Times*, April 26, 1878.
21. *Black Hills Daily Pioneer*, May 14, 1878.
22. *Daily Pioneer*, June 13, 1878; *Black Hills Daily Times*, June 14, 1878.
23. *Black Hills Daily Times*, February 17, 1880.
24. *Daily Times*, September 11, 1877.
25. *Daily Times*, August 20, 1878.
26. *Daily Times*, August 23, 1878.
27. *Daily Times*, November 6, 1877.
28. *Daily Times*, March 4, 1880.
29. *Daily Times*, December 12, 1878.
30. *Daily Times*, June 9, 1881.
31. *Black Hills Daily Pioneer*, July 25, 1878.
32. *Black Hills Daily Times*, February 28, 1882.
33. *Daily Times*, April 1, 1882.
34. *Daily Times*, August 2, 1883.
35. *Daily Times*, April 4, 1883.
36. *Black Hills Pioneer*, November 19, 1883.
37. *Black Hills Daily Times*, December 16, 1883.
38. *Daily Times*, February 1, 1885.
39. *Daily Times*, July 11, 1885.
40. *Daily Times*, July 19, 1885; July 21, 1885; July 22, 1885.
41. *Daily Times*, July 26, 1885.
42. *Daily Times*, October 14, 18, 1885.
43. *Omaha Daily Bee*, September 11, 1892.
44. *Daily Bee*, August 5, 1893.
45. *Omaha World Herald*, May 23, 1896.
46. *Daily Bee*, December 12, 1896.
47. *Daily Bee*, December 30, 1897.
48. *Omaha World Herald*, July 1, 1904.

Chapter 12 – Cynthia E. Cleveland: An Activist in the Dakotas

1. *National Society of the Daughters of the American Revolution*, Volume 14:10.
2. *Herringshaw's Encyclopedia of American Biography*, p. 226.

3. Cynthia Cleveland, *See-Saw* (University of Michigan Library, 1887), p. 19.
4. Personal communications with Jamie Karl, Administrative Director of the Oakland County Pioneer and Historical Society, in Pontiac Michigan. Cynthia E. Cleveland appears in the 1875 *Michigan State Gazetteer and Business Directory*.
5. U.S. Census, 1880, Michigan.
6. Swartz, 1900: p. 9.
7. *Black Hills Daily Times*, May 26, 1877.
8. *Black Hills Daily Times*, February 25, 1878.
9. *Black Hills Daily Times*, September 15, 1877; May 10, 1879.
10. *Black Hills Daily Times*, May 17, 1878.
11. *Black Hills Daily Times*, March 15, 1881.
12. *Black Hills Daily Times*, July 7, 1881.
13. *Black Hills Daily Times*, July 12, 1881.
14. *Black Hills Daily Times*, July 19, 1881.
15. *Black Hills Daily Times*, July 23, 1881.
16. *Black Hills Daily Times*, July 23, 1881.
17. *Black Hills Daily Times*, July 30, 1881.
18. *Black Hills Daily Times*, August 1, 1881.
19. *Black Hills Daily Times*, August 1, 1881.
20. *Black Hills Daily Times*, August 2, 1881.
21. *Black Hills Daily Times*, August 3, 1881.
22. *Black Hills Daily Times*, August 3, 1881.
23. *Black Hills Daily Times*, August 2, 1881.
24. *Black Hills Daily Times*, August 4, 1881.
25. *Black Hills Daily Times*, August 5, 6, 1881.
26. *Black Hills Daily Times*, August 6, 1881.
27. *Black Hills Daily Times*, August 8, 1881.
28. *Bismarck* (Dakota Territory) *Tribune*, August 19, 1881.
29. *Black Hills Daily Times*, August 12, 1881.
30. *Black Hills Daily Times*, August 17, 1881.
31. *Bismarck Tribune*, September 2, 1881.
32. *Black Hills Daily Times*, September 6, 1881.
33. *Bismarck Tribune*, September 2, 1881.
34. *Black Hills Daily Times*, November 4, 1881.
35. *Black Hills Daily Times*, November 9, 1881.

36. *Bismarck Tribune,* November 18, 1881.
37. *Black Hills Daily Times,* November 28, 1881.
38. *Black Hills Daily Times,* December 2, 1881.
39. *Black Hills Daily Times,* December 30, 1881.
40. *Black Hills Daily Times,* January 10, 1882.
41. Homestead claim of Cynthia E. Cleveland.
42. Swartz, 1900: p. 10.
43. (Pierre, Dakota Territory) *Evening Free Press,* June 3, 1884.
44. A flyer titled *Rare Bargains in Cynthia E. Cleveland's Addition to Highmore, Dakota.* This document is archived at the South Dakota State Historical Society Archives in Pierre, South Dakota.
45. *Washington Post,* February 18, 1884.
46. *Mitchell* (Dakota Territory) *Daily Republican,* December 4, 1887. In my research, this was the only indication of this activity. And it must be noted that the newspaper running the article was Republican and Cynthia was a dedicated Democrat.
47. *Dakota Journal,* May 7, 1884.
48. *Black Hills Daily Times,* October 25, 1882.
49. Cleveland, *See-Saw,* p. 20.
50. *Black Hills Daily Times,* April 6, 1883.
51. *Bismarck Tribune,* April 20, 1883.
52. (Chamberlain, Dakota Territory) *Dakota Register,* April 19, 1883.
53. (Burlington, Iowa) *Hawk Eye,* May 10, 1883.
54. Cleveland, *See-Saw,* p. 53.
55. (Pierre, Dakota Territory) *Dakota Journal,* August 3, 1883.
56. *Pierre City Directory,* July, 1883. Cynthia is listed under the heading of "Attorneys at Law."
57. It may have been the other way around, that the WCTU severed ties with Cynthia. There seemed to be much concern over her taking on a case that defended someone using or selling liquor. At any rate, the WCTU does not seem to play as large a role as does politics from this point on. After numerous calls to the WTCU archives in the 2003 and 2004, it has become painfully obvious that the organization does not wish to provide any information regarding Cynthia's relationship with it. It can only be

surmised that they also did not approve of her taking or winning the Adah Williams case.

58. *Dakota Journal*, August 3, 1883.
59. *Dakota Journal*, October 3, 1883.
60. *Dakota Journal*, October 10, 1883.
61. *Dakota Journal*, July 24, 1884.
62. *Twentieth Century Biographical Dictionary of Notable Americans*, Vol. II; *Dakota Journal*, Pierre, September 25, 1884.
63. *Traverse City* (Michigan) *Herald*, July 24, 1884.
64. Cleveland, *See-Saw*, p. 63.
65. (East Pierre, Dakota Territory) *Daily Evening Free Press*, February 13, 1885.
66. Cleveland vigorously pursued a policy barring special favors to any economic group, and I am sure that this is one of the things that Cynthia liked about Grover, but she still felt that he owed her something.
67. *Mitchell Daily Republican*, June 5, 1886.
68. *Black Hills Daily Times*, November 5, 1887.
69. *Black Hills Daily Times*, November 10, 1887.
70. *Mitchell Daily Republican*, December 4, 1887.
71. *Atchison Daily Globe*, November 9, 1887.
72. Cleveland, *See-Saw*, p. 67.
73. This is also a subject that was on the mind of President Cleveland, and he ordered the investigation of western lands that the railroads held by government grant. He forced railroads to return 81 million acres. He also signed the Interstate Commerce Act, the first law attempting federal regulation of the railroads.
74. *Atchison* (Kansas) *Daily Globe*, March 12, 1888.
75. *Mitchell Daily Republican*, November 2, 1887.
76. (Oshkosh, Wisconsin) *Daily Northwestern*, January 8, 1888.
77. *Mitchell Daily Republican*, February 21, 1890.
78. *Atlanta Constitution*, May 12, 1890.
79. *Washington, D.C. City Directory*, 1890.
80. *Mitchell Daily Republican*, March 11, 1890.
81. *Bismarck Tribune*, February 5, 1892.
82. *Stevens Point* (Wisconsin) *Gazette*, October 30, 1895.

83. *Atlanta Constitution*, October 24, 1895.
84. *Washington Post*, April 16, 1906.
85. *Washington Post*, January 22, 1916; February 15, 1917.
86. *Washington Post*, September 3, 1911.
87. Personal conversation on January 20, 2004, of Jerry L. Bryant with Mr. Tewodros Abebe, now Senior Archivist at Howard University, Washington, D.C.
88. Phone conversation on January 26, 2004, Jerry L. Bryant with Judy Lem-Sharp, U.S. Treasury Department Librarian. Her reference was the *Official Registry of the United States*.
89. *Washington Post*, March 11, 1932.

Chapter 13 – The Flormanns: In the Grip of Gold Fever

1. The case was summarized in the *Black Hills Weekly Times*, August 21, 1886.
2. "Tragedy in Red Canyon," *Deadwood Magazine*, Spring 2002, accessed at http://deadwoodmagazine.com, August 2015.
3. George W. Stokes, in collaboration with Howard R. Driggs, *Deadwood Gold: A Story of the Black Hills* (Chicago: World Book Co., 1925). Information attributed to Stokes in this chapter comes from his book. Flormann's "residence" at Claim No. 11 also was mentioned in the *Black Hills Pioneer*, September 23, 1876.
4. Lawrence County's first courthouse burned in the Great Fire of 1879. A rented building sufficed until 1889, when a two-story brick structure was erected. The third courthouse was dedicated on New Year's Day, 1908, and later contributed to creation of the Deadwood Historic District on the National Register of Historic Places. This building underwent extensive and necessary interior renovation and modernization in the 1990s. http://www.lawrence.sd.us/courthou1.htm.
5. *Black Hills Weekly Times*, April 22, 1877.
6. *Black Hills Daily Pioneer*, June 8, 1876.
7. *Black Hills Pioneer*, September 23, 1876.
8. *Black Hills Daily Pioneer*, October 7, 1876.
9. *Black Hills Pioneer*, February 17, 1877; February 28, 1879.

10. *Black Hills Daily Times*, February 3, 1877.
11. *Black Hills Weekly Times*, April 15, 1877.
12. *Black Hills Daily Times*, February 3, 1877.
13. *Daily Times*, May 5, 1877.
14. *Black Hills Champion*, October 27, 1877.
15. *Black Hills Daily Times*, April 14, 1879.
16. *Daily Times*, May 5, 1877.
17. *Black Hills Daily Times*, March 27, 1878.
18. *Daily Times*, November 14, 1879.
19. A "miner's inch" measures water volume combined with speed. Such an inexact measure could have meaning only in a certain location and season. Today, the miner's inch has been standardized for South Dakota and some other relatively dry U.S. states at 1/50th of a cubic foot of water flow per second. "Miner's inch," *Wikipedia: The Free Encyclopedia*, http://wikipedia.org, accessed September 2015.
20. *Black Hills Weekly Pioneer*, September 18, 1880.
21. *Black Hills Daily Times*, April 30, 1881.
22. For before-and-after photographs of the Windsor Block restoration, see http://www.stateline7.com/Projects/Windsor%20Block%20Lofts/Windsor_2.html.
23. David A. Wolff, "No Matter How You Do It, Fraud is Fraud: Another Look at Black Hills Mining Scandals," *South Dakota History*, Vol. 33, No. 2, p. 97. This excellent thirty-page article summarizes four scams: Greenwood Mining Company, Harney Peak Tin Company, Deadwood Reduction Works, and Horseshoe Mining Company. The authors are indebted to Dr. Wolff.
24. *Pierre* [Dakota] *Press*, reprinted in *Black Hills Weekly Times*, January 24, 1885.
25. *Black Hills Weekly Times*, May 17, 1885.
26. *Black Hills Weekly Times*, January 15, 1887.
27. From Reports of Cases Decided in the Supreme Court of the State of South Dakota. See: Tilton v. Flormann et al., pp. 324-340.
28. *Salt Lake Tribune*, June 26, 1899.

Chapter 14 – Young Jim: A Deadwood Waif

1. *Black Hills Champion,* August 27, 1877.

Chapter 15 – E. B. Farnum: Deadwood's First Mayor

1. United States Census, Walworth County, Wisconsin, 1870.
2. *Black Hills Daily Pioneer,* April 21, 1877.
3. *Daily Pioneer,* August 5, 1876.
4. *Daily Pioneer,* June 8, 1876.
5. *Daily Pioneer,* December 9, 1876.
6. *Daily Pioneer,* August 19, 1876.
7. *Daily Pioneer,* September 16, 1876.
8. *Daily Pioneer,* September 23, 1876.
9. *Daily Pioneer,* October 28, 1876.
10. *Daily Pioneer,* January 20, 1877.
11. *Black Hills Champion,* June 25, 1877.
12. *Black Hills Daily Pioneer,* January 6, 1877.
13. *Daily Pioneer,* November 18, 1876.
14. *Daily Pioneer,* November 25, 1876.

Chapter 16 – The First Decade of Deadwood's Public Schools: 1876-1886

1. *Black Hills Pioneer,* July 15, 1876.
2. *Pioneer,* November 11 and 18, 1876.
3. *Times-Picayune,* June 23, 1880.
4. *Black Hills Daily Times,* August 22, 1883.

Chapter 17 – The Telephone Comes to Deadwood

1. *Black Hills Daily Times,* March 11, 1878.

Chapter 18 – The Locomotive *J. B. Haggin*

1. Information from Adams Museum, 54 Sherman Street, Deadwood, SD 57732.

INDEX

(Page numbers in bold indicate photograph or illustration)

D

E

F

G

H

I

J

K

L

M

N

O

P

W

Y

ABOUT THE AUTHORS

Jerry L. Bryant

The late Jerry L. Bryant, a member of Registered Professional Archaeologists, was a historian with a passion for solving the riddles of Deadwood's past and preserving the Black Hills' historic sites and stories. As one of the foremost authorities in the life of Al Swearingen (collateral descendants prefer this spelling), Bryant was honored by the Academy of Television Arts and Sciences for his work on the HBO series Deadwood. Bryant held a bachelor's degree in anthropology and a master's in cultural resources management, working in that capacity for the U.S. Bureau of Land Management, the U.S. Forest Service, and the Adams Museum in Deadwood. He was also a decorated Navy veteran.

Barbara Fifer

Barbara Fifer majored in creative writing and comparative literature at Ohio University while working summers at a daily newspaper. She co-edited the Montana Historical Society's journal, *Montana: The Magazine of Western History* and has edited and written innumerable magazine articles and books, including the following Farcountry titles: *Wanted! Wanted Posters of the Old West; Montana Mining Ghost Towns; Montana Battlefields, 1806-1877; Going Along the Emigrant Trails; Going Along with Lewis & Clark;* and the *Lewis & Clark Expedition Illustrated Glossary*. Fifer continues to write and edit from her home in Helena, Montana.